THE
GOOD QUEEN
CHARLOTTE

THE GREAT HISTORY OF
THE QUEEN OF GREAT BRITAIN
AND WIFE OF GEORGE III

By

PERCY H. FITZGERALD

First published in 1899

Read & Co.

Copyright © 2023 Read & Co. History

This edition is published by Read & Co. History,
an imprint of Read & Co.

British Library Cataloguing-in-Publication Data
A catalogue record for this book is available
from the British Library.

Read & Co. is part of Read Books Ltd.
For more information visit
www.readandcobooks.co.uk

Percy H. Fitzgerald

A Biography by James Gibson

Born in 1834, at Fane Valley, County Louth, Ireland. Educated at Stonyhurst College, Lancashire, and Trinity College, Dublin, called to the Irish bar, and appointed a Crown Prosecutor on the North Eastern Circuit, author of various works of fiction, which originally appeared in *All the Year Sound, Dublin University Magazine*, and *Once a Week*. He has also written lives of Sterne, Garrick, Charles Lamb, the Kembles, Queen Charlotte, &c.

An excerpt from
The Bibliography of Robert Burns . . . , 1881

ABSTRACT OF CONTENTS

NOTE.

Since the earlier sheets of this work were printed, I have learned, on high authority, that the statement on page 60 as to the jewels "handed over to King George of Hanover," in 1857, is not exactly accurate—only a portion having been thus restored. The statement in the same page that Her present Majesty received a Jubilee present of emeralds from the Czar and Czarina, I am informed by the same authority, is also inaccurate.

P F.

Lemercier gravure

Printed in Paris

THE GOOD QUEEN CHARLOTTE

CHAPTER I.

THE YOUNG KING.

GEORGE III., who ascended the throne in 1760, was a youth of great promise and much sagacity. His mother, the Princess of Wales, who by the death of her husband had been deprived of the succession, had considerable influence over her child, and with the aid of Lord Bute, popularly considered "the Favourite," seemed to cherish ambitious dreams of wholly directing and controlling the Government. The long reign that was now opening with such fair hopes was destined to be a chequered one ; and it might be said that few persons in a private station who have been unlucky or unfortunate have encountered so many disasters and misfortunes. For a time, indeed, all went well and happily for this most domestic of monarchs. Not yet was he harassed by undutiful and rebellious children, who brought him discredit, or by the miserable tragedy of his sister in Denmark ; by turbulent and hostile politicians and ministers, who were opposed even to his sovereignty ; by the revolt and final loss of flourishing colonies ; by the general scandal of his daughter-in-law's proceedings ; or by his own recurring insanity, and final extinction of reason, as well as of sight. A more piteous story of royal suffering cannot be conceived. But now as the reign opened there were no prognostics of such disasters, and all seemed hopeful.

The young king was highly impressionable. It is an oft-told tale, that of his admiration for the beautiful Lady Sarah Lennox ; and there is the legend, for it is nothing more, of the young Quakeress, Hannah Lightfoot. It seems a strange thing, if it be true, that he should, even for a moment, have thought of placing a subject on the throne : he is reported, indeed, to have sent Lady Sarah a message " that an English match would be much better than a foreign one " ; but the thing could never have been entertained seriously, and the nation would certainly not have accepted it. It was probably no more than an ardent " flirtation," and the young king in the warmth of his affection—like many a young man of position—for the moment believed that he could give effect to his wishes and promises.

Lady Louisa Stuart had often heard Lady Macartney describe this curious scene : " At the court ball on his Majesty's birthday, June 4th, 1761, Lady Sarah's place was of course at the head of the dancers' bench, nearest his seat : the royal chair, heavy as it was, was moved nearer and nearer to the left, and he edged further and further the same way, and the conversation went on till all dancing was over and everybody sat in suspense ; and it approached one in the morning ere he recollected himself and rose to dismiss the assembly."

This vivacious lady, who heard much of the " ins and outs " of court intrigues, further tells us that her mother had often assured her " that no thought of marrying the young lady ever once entered into the king's head ; but in love with her he certainly was, and if she had played her cards well, there is no knowing what influence she might have had over him. Too young to be ambitious, she did not play them at all. One memorable day he accosted her with great *empressement* at the Drawing Room : she turned away, scarcely giving him an answer ; he then recollected he was a king, turned on *his* heel, and quitted her in visible displeasure."

From the first Lord Holland's MS., which Lady Louisa had seen, it is stated that " she gathered that his ambitious hopes had been raised and he thought there was a great stake either of her becoming wife, or all-powerful mistress, which was worth playing for, but she was not manageable." He gives an account of the scene at court just related, and then goes on to tell " what had put the young lady out of humour. There is a very foolish, idle boy, Lord Newbottle—Lady Sarah, in short, had had a quarrel with the lover she liked, had cried all night, and avenged his offence on the king, to her brother-in-law's extreme vexation. Lord Newbottle being the old lord of *your* day, idle enough, heaven knows, to the last, without the excuse of being foolish. He who had no passion but vanity cared not a straw for her."

One night long after the king's marriage, at the queen's house, Princess Elizabeth asked Lady Louisa it she thought her sister Mary was likely to be handsome, " for do you know papa says she will be like Lady Sarah Bunbury, who was the prettiest woman he ever saw in his life ? " She had evidently not heard of the old story. When Miss Napier, a daughter of Lady Sarah's, had been presented that day by her aunt, Lady Louisa Connolly, the king declared she was much the handsomest girl he had seen for a great while. The queen, like a true woman, looking by no means pleased, observed drily, " I wonder your Majesty should think so."

That the lady was likely to have been not very scrupulous is shown clearly by what occurred within a few years after this episode. She married Sir C. Bunbury, and, after a short time, " went off," as it was called, with Lord William Gordon. In this business she showed a heartlessness and absence of shame that scandalized even the lax society of the day. Her friend and " go-between," in her attempt to win the king, also ran off with an actor, O'Brien. His Majesty had therefore a lucky escape.

In the face of these rumours and the danger which might arise, the princess and the ministers thought it prudent to arrange as speedily as possible for the king's marriage. No time was lost contriving this important matter, and as was later done in the case of the Prince of

Wales, an agent was despatched abroad, who was to go round to the various German Courts, inspect the likely candidates, and report home. This practice, which seems odd enough, was necessary in those days of slow travel and long distances. It was, of course, out of the question that the suitor himself should leave his kingdom on a matrimonial expedition of the kind ; still, as may be imagined, under the system there was the chance of some later awkward surprise and disappointment : a painful example of which was to occur in the instance of George, Prince of Wales, who had to call for brandy to help him to recover from the first shock of the sight of his bride. There can be little doubt, however, that the choice had been all but made before his departure—one of the German princesses having attracted the king's notice in a rather romantic way.

The little principality of Strelitz was an interesting specimen of the old-fashioned and somewhat homely German dukedom, as described by Wraxall and other vivacious writers. Frederick, the third duke, was unmarried, and the next heir was his brother Charles Lewis, who, however, died before the reigning duke ; thus his son Adolphus Frederick became heir, and succeeded in 1751. His wife was the daughter of the Duke Saxe-Hilburg-hausen. He had two sisters and three brothers, and their modest revenues were about £15,000 a year—the income of a rather poor peer, as he would be con sidered in England. The whole territory was about 120 miles long by thirty in breadth.

The dowager duchess, though her husband had been succeeded by her son, was the head of the establishment, and was respectfully deferred to by the reigning duke, who was guided by her advice and great assistance. They all lived together like a happy family. Dr. Nugent, the amiable and popular member of the Literary Club, and Johnson's friend, visited many of these little German courts about the middle of last century, and gives a pleasing picture of the life at Strelitz.

The future queen, Sophia Charlotte, was born May 16th or May 19th, o.s. 1744. She was at this time about seventeen years old, and had been brought up in an unpretending way, like the daughter of a private gentleman, for during her childhood the chance of succeeding to the dukedom seemed remote. Nor do we hear at Strelitz of any of those scandals which then disgraced so many of the smaller German courts. She was carefully educated, knew many languages, was fond of botany and natural history, devoted to music : she was a good housewife, and skilful and laborious at her needle. Above all, she was reared in principles of the strictest piety and morality. She was deeply interested in the welfare of the peasants about her, and went among them, taking an interest in their condition.

The young princesses were first placed under the direction of a Madlle. Seltzer, a Wurtemberg lady ; but when the family came to live at Strelitz, the eldest girl being eighteen, the younger eight years old, a new governess was selected, Madame de Grabow, a lady of noble birth, daughter of the Minister from Mecklenburg at the Court of Vienna. She was now a widow and well off. She was known as "the German Sappho," from her many gifts and accomplishments. She knew Latin, could speak many languages, was "well up" in history, and, moreover, particularly skilled in the construction of maps, which "she drew with equal skill and accuracy." This taste she later imparted to her charges, the future queen being always conspicuous for her love of geography.

The children of the duke were all born at Mirow, a modest palace, or rather country house, in the duchy. They were brought up in the most careful way, receiving an admirable education, and being grounded in religious principles under the direction of an excellent mother. They were further directed by M. Gentzner, a Lutheran minister of many accomplishments, who had a particular knowledge of botany, mineralogy, and the kindred sciences. Her brother, when only fifteen, was appointed rector of one of the court universities, and delivered a Latin oration before the professors, which, however, was probably prepared for him in the customary way.

The daily life at Strelitz was nearly that of the family of some simple English country gentleman, only hardly so luxurious. The morning was devoted to study and instruction in needlework, embroidery, and lace-making, in which the daughters were very skilful. Queen Charlotte, as we know, had always her piece of work in hand. Then came a walk or drive, and at one o'clock the

dinner, which was always served in public, and with
much state and formality.   The rest of the day was then
free for amusements, excursions, etc.   At night there
were cards, music, and dancing, and about ten all went
to bed.   At Mecklenburg, we are told that "the princess lived in the greatest retirement, she dressed only
en robe de chambre, except on Sundays, on which day she
put on her best gown, and after service, which was very
long, took an airing in a coach and six, attended by
guards.   She was not yet, however, allowed to dine in
public."   It must have been an extraordinary surprise
for the simple girl to find herself called from this
pristine retirement to take her seat on the English
throne.

No one has given us so lively and graphic a sketch of
the old Strelitz life and the characters that figured
therein as Thomas Carlyle, who seems to have saturated
himself with the spirit of the innumerable memoirs and
chronicles which he read for his monumental life of
Frederick.   So odd and grotesque are the details in
these records, that they would be almost unintelligible
to the general reader, but for his quaint method of
interpretation.   He puts himself in the position of a
bystander or some contemporary German ; and in his
strange, half English, half foreign dialect, sets forth the
pith of the more significant passages.   He takes us back
some five or six and twenty years before to 1736, when
the young Frederick was living not far from Strelitz.

"It was Dowager Apanager (Wittwensitz), the widow of

the late Strelitz of blessed memory ; here, with her one child, a boy now grown to what manhood we see, has the serene dowager lived these twenty-eight years past, a Schwartzburg by birth, 'the cleverest head among them all.' Twenty-eight years in dilapidated Mirow; so long has *that tailoring duke*, her eldest stepson (child of a prior wife), been supreme head of Mecklenburg-Strelitz, employed with his needle. There was but one other son : this clever lady's—twenty years junior—Prince of Mirow ; Karl Ludwig Friedrich is the name of this one, age now twenty-eight the May 6th, 1708, when the Serene Father died, has been at Mirow with 'Mamma,' getting what education there was. Eight years before, in 1726, Mamma sent him off upon his travels to Geneva, and Italy and France ; he looked in upon Vienna too, got a lieutenant-colonelcy in the Kaiser's service, but did not like it, soon gave it up, and returned home to vegetate—perhaps to seek a wife, having prospects of succession in Strelitz. For if his serene half-brother proves to have no children, were his tailoring finished in the world, our Prince of Mirow is Duke-in-Chief. On this basis he wedded last year, that is, in 1736 ; the little wife has already brought him one child, a daughter, and has (as Friedrich notices) another under way if it prosper. No lack of daughters, nor of sons by-and-by. Eight years hence came the little Charlotte—subsequently Mother of England, much to her and our astonishment. The poor man did not live to be Duke of Strelitz; he died in 1752, in little Char-

lotte's eighth year, Tailor Duke surviving him a few
months.[1]

"Little Charlotte's brother did then succeed, and
lasted till 1794, after whom a second brother, father of
the now Serene Strelitzes—who is also genealogically
notable. For from him there came another still more
famous queen, Louise of Prussia; beautiful to look on, as
Aunt Charlotte was not, in a high degree, and who showed
herself a heroine in Napoleon's time, as Aunt Charlotte
never was called to do. Both aunt and niece were
women of sense, of probity, and propriety, fairly beyond
the average of queens. And as to their early poverty,
ridiculous to this gold nugget generation, I rather guess
it may have done them benefit, which the gold-nugget
generation, with its queens and otherwise, stands far
more in want of than it thinks."

Leaving here, for a moment, this odd account, with
its fantastical phrases, it may be worth while considering
in greater detail what a remarkable family this was,
deserving something higher, by way of presentation,
than Carlyle's odd nicknames.

Queen Charlotte's brother, the reigning prince, had
four daughters. The first, the most celebrated, was the

[1] It is surprising how a writer of Carlyle's acuteness and power
should have indulged in such freaks and antics as these about the
"Tailor Duke," "Tailoring Duke," etc., which went down marvel-
lously with the public in the "fifties," when the book came out, but
which reads with uncommon flatness and poverty now. The trick has
indeed no value at all, conveys nothing, not more than fixing a nick-
name on the person. For in this instance the "tailoring" was a mere
accident, an occasional thing, and not of the essence.

interesting and heroic Louise, Queen of Prussia, whose memory is still tenderly cherished, and whose beautiful face and figure is familiar in all lands through the well-known portrait. The second sister married Prince Louis, the King of Prussia's brother, a third the Prince of Tour and Taxis, and the fourth a prince of the house of Saxe-Hilbruchs-hausen. The aunt of all these princesses was, as we have seen, Queen Charlotte. One of her grand-nieces was to marry the King of Bavaria. These were influential alliances. The Princess Frederica, the second daughter, was destined to be the *enfant terrible* of the family, and her erratic proceedings brought much trouble to the closing years of the queen. This lady, on the death of her husband, Prince Louis of Prussia, speedily made a *mésalliance* with a certain Prince Solms, a remarkably handsome man, who was captain of a company of Dutch Guards. This union, strange to say, was favoured by the beautiful Queen Louise, no doubt from attachment to her sister, and though the king was much displeased, she contrived to reconcile him to the match, procuring from him a residence and an increase of pension with other favours. There were some five or six children of this marriage, and, when the queen was dying, one of her last requests to her husband was that he would take care of them. It was certainly creditable to the house of Mecklenburg-Strelitz that it should have furnished two such distin-guished personages as Queen Charlotte and her niece, Queen Louise. Though both exhibited the same sort of

courage and "grit" in moments of trial, their characters
were totally opposed. There was but little romance in
the aunt—at least, it lay deep beneath the surface—but
her nature was just as warm and affectionate.

Returning now to Carlyle's narrative, we find that in
October, 1736, the Crown Prince Friederich, who was
being kept strictly at Reinsberg by his father's orders,
one morning set off for the village and schloss in
Mecklenburg—known now as Mirow—to call on the
ducal family there.

The crown prince wrote an account of his visit to
his father on the next day. He rather humorously
described the castle, which he said reminded him of the
gardener's house at home, "only there is a rampart
round it, and an old tower, considerably in ruins, serves
as a gateway. Coming on the drawbridges, I perceived
an old stocking-knitter disguised as a grenadier, with his
cap, cartridge-box, and musket laid aside that they might
not hinder his knitting." He describes how he was
interrogated by the sentry as to whence he came and
whither he was going, of which challenge he took no
heed, but went on to the schloss. "Never in my life
should I have taken this for a schloss but for the two
glass lamps and the figures of two cranes standing in
front by way of guards. We made up to the house, and
after knocking almost half an hour to no purpose, there
peered out at last an exceedingly old woman, who looked
as if she might have nursed the prince of Mirow's father.
She was so terrified that she slammed the door in our

faces. We knocked again, and seeing that nothing
could be made of it, went round to the stables, where a
fellow told us that the prince and his retinue had gone
off to pay a visit at New Strelitz, and the duchess, his
mother, had sent with him all her people, so as to make
a good show, keeping no one but the old woman." The
prince thought the best thing to do was to follow them,
and have a look at New Strelitz. He described it as no
more than a village with a single street in it, where
the chamberlains, officials, and domestics resided. The
castle struck him as fine, and was on a lake. The
prince of Mirow, however, was not at home, had
gone off to visit some other place. One of the
chamberlains told them that "the Duke of Strelitz was
an excellent seamstress, fit to be tailor to your majesty
in a manner, had not fate been cruel; that he made
beautiful dressing-gowns with his needle. I cannot
better describe the duke than by saying he is like old
Stahl in a blonde abbé's periwig. He is extremely silly :
his Hofrath tells him, as it were, everything he has to
say." Later he proceeded to the residence at Mirow
and saw the whole family. "The mother is a princess
of Schwartzenberg, and still the cleverest of them all.
The lady spouse is small; she was in the family way, but
seemed otherwise to be a very good princess. General
Praetorius was in his room when I entered with
the prince of Mirow : at sight of him Praetorius
exclaimed loud enough to be heard by everybody,
' *Voilà le Prince Cajuca!*' Not one of us could help

laughing : and I had my own trouble to turn it so that he did not get angry. Scarce was the prince got in, when they came to tell me that Prince Heinrich, the Margraf, was come, who accordingly trotted him out in such a way that we thought we should all have died with laughing. Incessant praises were given him, especially. for his fine clothes, his fine air, and his uncommon agility.

" The first thing they entertained me with was the sad misfortune come upon their best cook : who, with the cart that was bringing the provisions, had been overset, and had broken his arm : so that the provisions had all gone to nothing. Privately I have had inquiries made— there was not a word of truth in the story. At last we went to table : and sure enough it looked as if the cook and his provisions had come to some mishap, for certainly in the Three Crowns at Potsdam there is better eating.

" At table there was talk of nothing but of all the German princes who are not right in their wits—as Mirow himself, your majesty knows, is reputed to be. There was Weimar, Gotha, Waldeck, Hoym, and the whole lot brought on the carpet : and after our good host had got considerably drunk, he lovingly promised me that he and his whole family would come to visit me. Come he certainly will : but how I shall get rid of him, God knows.

" In the afternoon, to spoil his fine coat, we stepped out to shoot at targets in the rain ; he would not speak of it, but we observed he was in much anxiety about the coat. In the evening he got a glass or two in his head, and grew extremely merry : said at last, he was sorry, but for divers state reasons and businesses he must of necessity return home, which, however, he put off till about two in the morning. I think next day he would not remember very much of it."

This sketch furnishes a good idea of the rude and coarse atmosphere of these courts, with their rustic figures on a background of extravagance. It is a good introduction to the young bride.

The almost pastoral happiness of the little court at Strelitz had been rudely disturbed by the wars between the great Frederick and the Empress Maria Theresa, which was to prove disastrous for the small German territories, which he overran with his armies and pillaged and laid waste. His excuse was that they would not join him in the contest. The little Duchy of Mecklenburg-Strelitz suffered cruelly : contributions were levied, the young men were forced into the king's army, furniture and property plundered ; even the churches were despoiled. After the great defeat of Daun at Torgau in 1760 the whole of Germany seemed to be at the conqueror's mercy : so desperate was the outlook, that an extraordinary step was taken by the second of the young princesses then at Strelitz, and which was to determine her future destiny. As the victory seemed to portend a new series of horrors and despoilings, she addressed an earnest letter to Frederick, describing the sufferings of her country and appealing to his mercy and forbearance. This was an exceptional step in one so young—she was then only sixteen—and was as timely as it was efficacious. One might at first be inclined to doubt the truth of the story, for there is a melodramatic tone about it, and nothing is more common than such imaginary letters of sovereigns to other personages, which found their way into newspapers and memoirs. But this is thoroughly well authenticated by Lord Mahon in his History, and by various German writers.

The letter ran :

" May it please your Majesty,

"I am at a loss whether I should congratulate or condole with you on your late victory, since the same success which has covered you with laurels has overspread the country of Mecklenburg with desolation. I know, sire, that it seems unbecoming my sex, in this age of vicious refinement, to feel for one's country, to lament the horrors of war, or to wish for the return of peace. I know you may think it more properly my province to study the arts of pleasing, or to inspect subjects of a more domestic nature ; but, however unbecoming it may be in me, I cannot resist the desire of interceding for this unhappy people.

" It was but a very few years ago that this territory wore the most pleasing appearance. The country was cultivated, the peasant looked cheerful, and the towns abounded with riches and festivity. What an alteration at present from such a charming scene. I am not expert at description, nor can my fancy add any horrors to the picture ; but surely even conquerors themselves would weep at the hideous prospects now before me. The whole country, my dear country, lies one frightful waste, presenting only objects to excite terror, pity, and despair. The employments of the husbandman and the shepherd are quite suspended ; for the husbandman and the shepherd are become soldiers themselves, and help to ravage the soil which they formerly cultivated. The towns are inhabited only by old men, women, and children ; while perhaps here and there a warrior, by wounds or loss of limbs rendered unfit for service, is left at his door, where his little children hang round him, ask the history of every wound, and grow themselves soldiers before they find strength for the field. But this were nothing, did we not feel the alternate insolence of either army as it happens to advance or retreat, in pursuing the operations of the campaign. It is impossible, indeed, to express the confusion which they who call themselves our friends create, for even those from whom we might expect relief only oppress us with new calamities. From your justice therefore, it is, sire, that we hope redress : to you even children and women may complain, whose humanity stoops to the meanest petition, and whose power is capable of repressing the greatest wrong."

It was noted that almost immediately after this letter was despatched, a complete change took place in the Prussian king's system. A missive to General de Ziethen enjoined order and regularity in the conduct of the army.

"I am determined," he wrote, " that henceforth all violent expedients, all exactions, all arbitrary supplies shall cease." Strict discipline was henceforth to be enforced. The king, indeed, was so pleased with the young princess and her appeal, that the letter was shown and handed about; a copy found its way to the English court and to the Princess of Wales, by whom it was shown to the king, who was greatly struck by it.

When the subject of the young monarch's marriage came on the *tapis*, and the court was busy with the selection of a bride, this letter became an important factor. The good sense and feeling exhibited in it, and its success as a piece of diplomacy, showed that the writer must have "character." It would therefore seem, though it is not quite certain, that the letter itself may have suggested the marriage.

CHAPTER II.

THE person selected for this delicate office of choosing a wife was Colonel Græme, or Graham—a notorious Jacobite who had been actually " out " in the '45, so that Hume's jest on him seemed well founded : that he had exchanged the dangerous office of making a king for the more lucrative one of making a king's marriage. Lord Bute's passion for employing his own countrymen was no doubt the reason of this selection, but Græme seems to have been a cautious, discreet man. The princess dowager, it was said, would have preferred one of the Brunswick princesses, but her choice was not found acceptable.[1]

Græme accordingly set off, and in due time appeared in the little court of Mecklenburg-Strelitz. On his arrival he found that the grand duchess and her two daughters were at the watering-place of Pyrmont, to which he followed, where they were seen as simple,

---

[1] Another suggested candidate was a princess of Hesse, who had been seriously thought of for the king, but there were such stories about her conduct that " nobody could take upon them to recommend her." (Thus the Duchess of Brunswick to Lord Malmsbury).

homely folk, frequenting the rooms, and following the tranquil amusements of the place. He had thus opportunities of studying the future bride under very favourable conditions, and was more than satisfied with what he saw. She was, however, not by any means a beauty, and the emissary reported only moderately of her looks. An acute observer, Walpole, described her later :—"Her person," he said, "was small and 'very lean,' not well made ; her face, pale and homely, her nose somewhat flat, and mouth *very large.* Her hair, however, was of a fine brown, and her countenance pleasing. She had an unfailing good humour and animation, which supplied for these defects." In the National Portrait Gallery is a flamboyant full length by Gainsborough, done some years later when she was in her prime, and which corresponds with the description, particularly in the large mouth and small face. In dealing with persons of such high degree there is a certain reserve, but an ordinary lady with the same features would be described as "snub-nosed," and perhaps as decidedly plain. Her features, however, were such as would improve with time, and an old Colonel Disbrowe, who was long about her court, once said humorously to Mr. Croker, "I do think that the *bloom* of *her ugliness* is going off." And it must be added indeed that Queen Caroline and Queen Adelaide were not the most favourable specimens of German good looks. The Princess Charlotte, the regent's daughter, was certainly handsome : her gracious Majesty on her accession was a beautiful and interesting creature, and her daughter-in-law, the ever-popular Princess of Wales, is one of the most attractive ladies of our time. All agreed, too, that any defects in the future queen were more than redeemed by her admirable good sense and good nature, and this, as Walpole said, " set off by much grace in her manner recommended all she said." There is, however, a much more favourable account given of the princess by one who knew her very well. " She was certainly not a beauty," writes Mrs. Papendieck, the wife of one of her attendants, " but her countenance was expressive and intelligent. She was not tall, but of a slight, rather pretty figure ; her eyes bright and sparkling with good-humour and vivacity, her mouth large, but filled with white and even teeth, and her hair really beautiful." Of course, the family at Strelitz knew what was the Colonel's errand. We are told he conducted the business " in the most private manner." He came home and duly made his report, which was at once acted upon, but speaking, as we have seen, " only moderately " of her looks.

On July 8th, 1761, the privy councillors were summoned to meet, and were duly mystified by the terms of the message, which spoke of " urgent and important business," marked also as " an absolute secret." It was thought that a peace or some other momentous matter was to be discussed. It proved to be the king's marriage. The meeting was a very full one, and this announcement was made public :—

" Having nothing so much at heart as to procure the

welfare and happiness of my people, and to render the
same stable and permanent to posterity, I have, ever
since my accession to the throne, turned my thoughts
towards the choice of a princess for my consort ; and I
now, with great satisfaction, acquaint you, that after the
fullest information and mature deliberation, I am come
to a resolution to demand in marriage the Princess
Charlotte of Mecklenburg-Strelitz, a princess distinguished by every eminent virtue and amiable endowment, whose illustrious line has constantly shown the
firmest zeal for the Protestant religion, and a particular
attachment to my family.

"I have judged proper to communicate to you these
my intentions, in order that you may be fully apprised of
a matter so highly important to me and to my kingdoms,
and which, I persuade myself, will be most acceptable to
all my loving subjects."

It seems a little strange that at this stage the project
should, at the request of the Council, have been at once
communicated to the public. The king, it will be seen,
openly announced his intention of asking the princess's
hand ; but of course there had been previous communication and the consent of the family assured.

Among those who had been summoned to the Privy
Council to hear the announcement of the intended
marriage was Lord Harcourt of Nuneham—a nobleman
who had been living somewhat in retirement. After the
meeting he was sent for by Lord Bute, and informed that
he had been appointed Master of the Horse, and was to

go on a special mission to Strelitz to convey the royal proposals. The king remarked to him that he was one of the few, perhaps the only man of quality, that had not solicited some favour of him upon his accession to the crown, that he had taken notice of it and was pleased. " After what happened to me some years ago," says Lord Harcourt, " it was beneath me to become a solicitor for favours. This honour I expected about as much as I did the Bishoprick of London, then vacant." [1] He presently had an audience of the king and received his formal commission. This was a fortunate choice, for Lord Harcourt and various members of his family were here- after destined to be the warmest and most valuable friends the king ever had. A later Lady Harcourt was regarded not only by the king and queen, but by all the princesses, as a cherished and valuable friend, and the intimacy was only dissolved by death.

On August 17th, 1761, the envoy wrote an account of his reception at the Mecklenburg Court to his friend Mitchell (later Sir Andrew Mitchell). It gives a pleasing sketch of the young princess :—

"Strelitz, Aug. 17, 1761.

" DEAR MITCHELL,—How unfortunate I am to lose the pleasure of introducing you to the most amiable

[1] *Ellis' original letters.* It will be understood that many of the details concerning the court and the Harcourt family are taken from the Harcourt papers, privately printed in many volumes by the late Mr. Edward Harcourt, of Nuneham ; no very special references therefore will be made to them.

young princess I ever saw. You may imagine what a reception I have met with at this court, coming upon opportunity of meeting you at Perleberg ; but am still more concerned for the accident that has deprived me of such an errand as brought me here, where the great honour the king has done this family is seen in its proper light.

" I reached this place on the 14th; on the 15th the treaty was concluded and despatched away to England. *L'affaire, en vérité, n'était pas bien épineuse.* This little Court exerted its utmost abilities to make a figure suitable to the occasion, and I can assure you they have acquitted themselves not only with magnificence and splendour, but with a great deal of good taste and propriety. Our queen that is to be has seen very little of the world, but her good sense, vivacity, and cheerfulness, I daresay, will recommend her to the king and make her the darling of the British nation. She is no regular beauty, but she is of a very pretty size, has a charming complexion, very pretty eyes, and finely made ; in short, she is a fine girl."

For his services on this conspicuous mission Earl Harcourt was handsomely remunerated. On August 5th, 1761, a warrant was issued directing the payment of £4000 to the envoy, " to allow him the sum for his journey to and from Mecklenburg-Strelitz, and for his trouble and expenses in the execution of his Majesty's commission. Appointing the said Earl to negotiate, conclude, and sign a treaty of marriage between his

Majesty and her Serene highness Princess Charlotte, and attending the said Princess to this Kingdom."

Mr. Walpole was rather satirical on this embassy, writing to a friend that Lord Harcourt was to go to the Court of Mecklenburg "*if he can find it.*" The earl was entrusted with the king's present, a miniature "richly set round with diamonds and a diamond rose."

A month later the formal embassy set forth to bring home the bride. The *Carolina* yacht was fitted up magnificently. Three very distinguished ladies were appointed to go out also, as ladies of the bedchamber ; these were the Duchess of Hamilton, one of the beautiful Gunnings, the Duchess of Ancaster, and Lady Effingham. A royal squadron under Lord Anson was despatched to Stade to await and escort the future bride home. On August 8th the party sailed, and by the 14th, in barely a week's time, arrived at Strelitz. Next morning Lord Harcourt was introduced, and, it is said, found the young princess sewing. There was a story circulated that she was surprised darning a pair of stockings, which a chronicler oddly says "was not surprising, when we consider the then distracted state of her country."

Lord Harcourt then formally made his proposals, the young lady listening without laying aside her work—a simplicity which must have pleased the envoy. The next stage was the contract and the odd ceremonial of the " marriage by proxy." One of her attendants[1] thus

[1] Later, Mrs. Papendieck.

graphically describes the scene :—"One morning her
eldest brother, of whom she seems to have stood in great
awe, came to her room in company with the duchess,
her mother. In a few minutes the folding-doors flew
open to the saloon, which she saw splendidly illuminated,
and then appeared a table, two cushions, and everything
prepared for a wedding. Her brother gave her his
hand, and, leading her in, used his favourite expression, '*Allons, ne fais pas l'enfant; tu vas être Reine
d'Angleterre.*'"

The formal betrothal by proxy then took place, Mr.
Drummond taking the place of the bridegroom. He
advanced, and they knelt down together. She was laid
upon her sofa, upon which he placed his foot ; and the
family all embraced her, calling her "La Reine." Mr.
Drummond was no doubt the English representative at
the little court, and acted in right of his position. Then
followed congratulations from the deputies of the towns
and "the states," and general festivities.

There was one curious incident connected with this
alliance : the future queen had an elder sister, the
Princess Christina, and the Duke of Roxburghe, being
on his travels and chancing to stop at Mecklenburg, had
formed an attachment to her, which was returned. It
was likely that a marriage would have taken place, but
unluckily the greater alliance came "on the carpet"
just at the critical moment. It was one of the stipula-
tions of the contract that no member of the family
should wed an English subject, and the enamoured

couple had to forego their design. Both died unmarried. The duke devoted himself to bibliography and rare books.

High festivities now followed on the betrothal. After receiving the congratulations and addresses of the various states and public bodies, a grand banquet was given at the palace, when, according to etiquette, the bride-elect dined at a separate table with Princess Schwartzenburg, her grand-aunt, and her sister. The grand duke entertained the English envoy and some of the high nobility at a separate table in the great saloon; while other tables were laid for a hundred and fifty covers. At night the gardens were lit up with 40,000 lamps, and the town was also illuminated. The next day was devoted to general festivities and rejoicings, and the day following, August 17th, was that of departure. A long procession of many carriages set out, with Lord Harcourt and his son in a coach and six, the cavalcade consisting of some thirty coaches. Unfortunately, the weather was stormy, and great gales were blowing, and it seemed uncertain at what time the nuptial party could be expected in England. The day for the coronation had been actually fixed and was close at hand. It was all-important, therefore, that the bride should arrive without delay. Fresh instructions from the king reached Stade that the party should depart at once, and the poor bride had to prepare herself for a stormy voyage. At Stade she was met by her new ladies, the Duchesses of Hamilton and Ancaster, who

knelt to her, whom she greeted with the pretty
speech that "she hoped friendship might take the
place of ceremony in their relations." Delighted with
the salutes, firing of cannon and ringing of bells, she
exclaimed, naturally enough, "And am I worthy of all
these honours?"

During the storm, when all her companions were in
agonies of suffering, the cheerful princess, with her sound
German constitution, was not in the least affected. A
harpsichord had been put on board for her use, and on
this she would play them gay tunes. Already she began
to show her independent character. The English ladies
gave her some hints, and suggested she should arrange
her hair in the English fashion. But she would not
hear of it. She would keep her own style, which, she
said, looked as well as that of her ladies. "If the king
desires me to wear a periwig, I will do so ; but until he
says so, I will be as I am." This was lively enough. The
ladies also told her that the king liked a particular sort
of dress. "Let him dress himself as he likes," she
answered smartly ; "I'll dress as I please." And as to
keeping early hours, "she had no notion of going to bed
with the fowls "—*se coucher avec les poules.*

At three in the afternoon, on Monday, September 7th,
the bride-elect first set foot on English ground at
Harwich, where she was received by the mayor and
aldermen of the corporation in all their formalities, amidst
an immense assemblage of persons of all ranks, who
hailed her appearance with loud acclamations. About

five o'clock the same day she came to Colchester, where
she stopped, and took tea at the house of Mr. Enew :
while there, she received a box of eringo root, the
product of that town, and which, according to ancient
custom, is always presented to any of the royal family
who visit that place. From Colchester she proceeded
to Witham, the seat of Lord Abercorn, who was not
present to do the honours of his house to so illustrious a
guest. However, as elegant an entertainment was provided as the time would permit ; and during supper
the door of the room was left wide open, that all persons
might have the pleasure of seeing their future queen ;
on one side of whose chair stood the Earl of Harcourt,
and on the other Lord Anson. The next morning, a
little after twelve o'clock, she came to Rumford, where
she alighted, and took coffee at the house of Mr. Dutton,
a wine merchant. At Rumford she was met by the
king's servants ; and about one o'clock entered his
Majesty's coach with the Duchesses of Ancaster and
Hamilton. She was now dressed entirely in the English
fashion, having a fly cap, with rich laced lappets, a
stomacher ornamented with diamonds, and a gold
brocade suit, with a white ground. Her coach was
preceded by three of the royal carriages, in which were
the several ladies of her suite, both English and German.
Perceiving the eagerness manifested by the people, who
thronged the roads as she passed, to have a view of her
person, she expressed her desire that the pace might be
moderated, to gratify public curiosity, while, at intervals,

she bowed most courteously to those who greeted her approach. The whole of her behaviour indicated a most agreeable temper; and every one who had an opportunity of observing her manner was quite charmed with the gracefulness of her deportment and the strong tokens of sensibility and goodness which appeared in her countenance.

Parties of the Leicestershire militia were posted in all the towns through which she had to pass ; and at Mile End she was met by the Life Guards, who accompanied her the remainder of the way.

She used to recall the agitating drive through London : and when passing up along Constitution Hill that one of her ladies—no doubt the downright Duchess of Hamilton—said, looking at her watch, " We shall hardly have time to dress for the wedding." " The wedding ! " exclaimed the queen. " Yes, madam ; it is to be at twelve (midnight)." Upon this she fainted. Lady Effingham had a bottle of lavender-water in her hand, and threw it in her face, and almost immediately her carriage stopped at the gate.

In all proceedings of this time it is impossible to do without the help of the vivacious and observing Horace Walpole, whose letters, full of lively detail, do duty over and over again in the memoirs. He thus wrote to Lord Strafford :—

" Nothing," says Mr. Walpole, " was ever equal to the bustle and uncertainty of the town for these three days. The queen was seen off the coast on Saturday last, and is not arrived yet ; nay, last night, at ten o'clock, it was neither certain where she landed nor when she would be in town. I forgive history for knowing nothing, when so public an event as the arrival of a new queen is a mystery even at this very moment in St. James's Street. The messenger that brought the letter yesterday morning said she *arrived* at half an hour after four at Harwich. This was immediately translated into *landing*, and notified in those words to the ministers. Six hours afterwards it proved no such thing, and that she was only in Harwich Road : and they recollected that *half an hour after four* happen twice in twenty-four hours, and the letter did not specify which of the *twices* it was. Well ! the bridemaids whipped on their virginity ; the New Road and the parks were thronged ; the guns were choaking with impatience to go off, and Sir James Lowther, who was to pledge his Majesty, was actually married to Lady Mary Stuart. Five, six, seven, eight o'clock came, and no queen. She lay at Witham, at Lord Abercorn's, who was most tranquilly in town ; and it is not certain even whether she will be composed enough to be in town to-night." This was on September 8th.

When the cavalcade drew up before the small private garden-gate of the Palace, she was welcomed by the Duke of York. The next moment she was before a large group—the king, his great officers, and ladies. It was an agitating scene for all. It was said indeed that the young creature, seeing a cushion before the old Duke of Grafton, was on the point of kneeling to him. She then attempted to kneel to the king, but he checked her and kissed her hand. No wonder that she was observed to tremble as she met all the grand personages. Yet when the free-and-easy Duchess of Hamilton smiled at her— "You may laugh," the young princess said smartly; "you have been married twice, but it is no joke for me."

After this meeting she was taken at once to see that great lady, the princess dowager, who received her attended by her daughters. They brought her to the rooms in the palace where the magnificent trousseau was laid out. In the "great wardrobe" room, as it was called, a staff of dressmakers were waiting to "fit on" and alter, etc., in hot haste, as might be necessary. Indeed, there was but little time; for the wedding was to take place that night, and much more was to be got over between.

Then came a state dinner. It was noticed that she had been a little confused and agitated during all these incidents, and how natural! but now she had quite resumed her cheerfulness "and recruited her peculiar sweetness of manner, which, combined with an interesting and expressive countenance, now seemed to touch the heart of the king. He had, indeed, though prepared by Græme's account, been a little disappointed at the first sight of the bride, but when she had gone to dress for the ceremony, he in a very natural way told his family that he already felt a great affection for her."

At nine o'clock (September 8th) the ceremony took place in the Chapel Royal, and was performed by the

Archbishop of Canterbury. The pleasant good-humour of the bride never deserted her for a moment. When she was told to kiss the peeresses she seemed pleased, but when she saw the long trains of bridesmaids, she seemed taken aback. " Mon Dieu," she cried, " such a number of kisses ! " There was a train of ten bridesmaids, at the head of which was Lady Sarah Lennox, with whom were the Ladies Caroline Russell, Caroline Montague, Harriet Bentinck, Anne Hamilton, E. Kerr, Elizabeth Keppel, Louisa Greville, Elizabeth Harcourt, and Susan Fox Strangways. They were sumptuously arrayed in satin, and bore the bride's train. The latter was bending under the weight of her magnificence and the weight of her jewels. She wore " an endless mantle " of rich violet and purple velvet, lined with ermine, over a white satin and silver dress. It was noticed that this ponderous mantle, which " was attempted to be fastened on her shoulders by a bunch of pearls, dragged itself and almost the rest of her clothes half way down her waist." But the jewels — a tiara of diamonds, a necklet, and a stomacher said to be worth £90,000, must have made a dazzling show indeed.

After the ceremony the party returned to the drawing-room, and supper being quite ready, the new queen gaily sat down to the harpsichord, no doubt to the surprise of the guests, and sang and played. At the banquet they sat on and on till three or four in the morning, until the Duke of Cumberland plainly hinted that he was dying with sleep. There used to be in those days some too familiar proceedings on the part of the guests, which the sensible and prudent young queen had stipulated should not be attempted on this occasion.

Levées and Drawing Rooms began on the very next day ; the new queen standing by the throne, the Duchess of Hamilton presenting the ladies. As her Majesty literally knew nobody, she could address nobody. An amusing incident was talked of.   Lord Westmoreland, who was old and near-sighted, mistook Lady Sarah Lennox for the queen, and knelt to her—he would have kissed her hand only she prevented it.   The celebrated Kitty Dashwood. so tunefully sung by the poet Hammond, was installed at the palace as a sort of duenna to her Majesty.

CHAPTER III.

THE marriage and its ceremonial being thus despatched in this prompt fashion, the general excitement was now turned in the direction of the grand ceremonial—the coronation—which was now impending. This function more particularly concerns the king's life, and has been often described. It took place on September 22nd, and was carried out with the customary magnificence. Mr. Walpole supplies us with the courtier's view.

"Some of the peeresses were dressed over night, slept in arm-chairs, and were waked if they tumbled their heads. I carried my Lady Townshend, Lady Hertford, Lady Anne Conolly, my Lady Hervey, and Mrs. Clive, to my deputy's house, at the gate of Westminster Hall. My Lady Townshend said she should be very glad to see a coronation, as she never had seen one. 'Why,' said I, 'Madam, you walked in the last.' 'Yes, child,' said she, 'but I saw nothing of it ; I only looked to see who looked at me.'"

In a letter to Mr. George Montague, the same pleasant writer observes : "The multitudes, balconies, guards, and processions, made Palace-Yard the liveliest spectacle in the world ; the Hall was the most glorious. The blaze of lights, the richness and variety of habits, the ceremonial, the benches of peers and peeresses, frequent and full, was as awful as a pageant can be ; and yet for the king's sake and my own I never wish to see another; nor am impatient to have my Lord Effingham's promise fulfilled. The king complained that so few precedents were kept for their proceedings."

To the Countess of Aylesbury he writes still more pleasantly : "My heraldry was much more offended at the coronation with the ladies that did walk, than with those that walked out of their place ; yet I was not so *perilously* angry as my Lady Cowper, who refused to set a foot with my Lady M—— ; and when she was at last obliged to associate with her, set out on a round trot, as if she designed to prove the antiquity of her family, by marching as lustily as a maid of honour of Queen Gwinevir. It was in truth a brave sight. The sea of heads in Palace-Yard, the guards, horse and foot, the scaffolds, balconies, and procession, exceeded imagination. The hall when once illuminated was noble ; but they suffered the whole parade to return into it in the dark that his Majesty might be surprised with the quickness with which the sconces catched fire. The champion acted well ; the other paladins had neither the grace nor alertness of Rinaldo. Lord Effingham and the Duke of Bedford were but untoward knights-errant ; and Lord Talbot had not much more dignity than the figure of

General Monk in the abbey. The habit of the peers is
unbecoming to the last degree : but the peeresses made
amends for all defects. Your daughter Richmond, Lady
Kildare, and Lady Pembroke, were as handsome as the
graces. Lady Rochford, Lady Holderness, and Lady
Lyttleton, looked exceedingly well in that their day ;
and for those of the days before, the Duchess of Queensberry, Lady Westmorland, and Lady Albemarle, were
surprising. Lady Harrington was noble at a distance,
and so covered with diamonds, that you would have
thought she had bid somebody or other, like Falstaff,
' rob me the exchequer.' Lady Northampton was very
magnificent too, and looked prettier than I have seen her
of late. Lady Spenser and Lady Bolingbroke were not
the worst figures there. The Duchess of Ancaster
marched alone, after the Queen, with much majesty ;
and there were two new Scotch peeresses that pleased
everybody, Lady Sutherland and Lady Dunmore. Per
contra, were Lady P. who had put a wig on ; and old E.
who had scratched her's off ; Lady S. the dowager E.
and a Lady S. with her tresses coal black, and her hair
coal white. Well, it was all delightful, but not half so
charming as its being over. The gabble one heard about
it for six weeks before, and the fatigue of the day, could
not well be compensated by a mere puppet show ; for
puppet show it was, though it cost a million." [1]

[1] The great cream-coloured horses, also an attraction at the recent
Jubilee, figured in the show. These so-called Hanoverian animals
are said to be a sort of Danish breed, formed by crossing grey English
mares with white Würtemburgs.

Another interesting ceremonial in which the new queen took a prominent part was a state visit to the City. In Cheapside, opposite Bow Church, was the house of the Barclays, worthy Quakers, where their Majesties remained several hours to see the civic procession go by. One of the ladies of this family wrote an account of the incidents of the visit to a friend at Warwick. It gives a very pleasing picture of the simple manners and *bonhomie* of the royal bride.

" As the royal family came, they were conducted into one of the counting-houses, which was transformed into a very pretty parlour for that purpose. A platform was raised in the street, on which, before their Majesties alighted, my brothers spread a carpet; and as soon as they entered, the procession began. The Queen came up first, handed by her chamberlain; the King followed, with the rest of the royal family, agreeable to their rank; the master and mistress of the house, and then the quality. On the second pair of stairs was placed our own company, about forty in number, the chief of whom were of the Puritan order, and all in their orthodox habits. Next the drawing-room door was placed our own selves, I mean my papa's children, for, to the great mortification of our visitors, none else were allowed to enter the drawing-room; for as kissing the King's hand without kneeling was an honour never before conferred, his Majesty chose to confine that mark of condescension to our own family, as a return for the trouble we had been at upon the occasion. But to proceed. After the royal pair had shown themselves to the populace for a few moments from the balcony, we were all introduced; and you may believe at that juncture we felt no small palpitations.

"His Majesty met us at the door, which was a condescension we did not expect; at which place he saluted us with great politeness; and advancing to the upper end of the room, we performed the ceremony of kissing the Queen's hand, at the sight of whom we were all in raptures, not only from the brilliancy of her appearance, which was pleasing beyond description; but being throughout her whole person possessed of that inexpressible something that is beyond a set of features, and equally claims our attention. To be sure, she has not a fine face, but a most agreeable countenance, and is vastly genteel, with an air, notwithstanding her being a little woman, truly majestic; and I really think by her manner, is expressed that complacency of disposition which is perfectly amiable; and though I could never perceive that she deviated from that dignity which belongs to a crowned head, yet on the most trifling occasions she displayed all that easy behaviour that elegant negligence can bestow. Her hair, which is of a light colour, hung in what is called coronation ringlets, encompassed with a circle of diamonds, so beautiful in themselves, and so prettily disposed, as will admit of no description : her clothes, which were as rich as gold, silver and silk could make them, was a suit from which fell a train, supported by a little page in scarlet and silver. The lustre of her

stomacher was inconceivable, being one of the presents
she received whilst Princess of Mecklenburg, on which
was represented, by the vast profusion of diamonds
placed on it, the magnificence attending so great a king;
and nothing could have added to the scene, but that
of conversing with the Queen, who inquired if we
could talk French for that purpose ; and so flattered
our vanity as to tell the lady-in-waiting that the
greatest mortification she had met with since her
arrival in England, was her not being able to converse
with us.

"As both the doors of the drawing-room were open
the whole time, the people without had a very good
opportunity of seeing ; besides which, the Queen was
up stairs three times; and one of these opportunities was
made use of for introducing my little darling, with Patty
Barclay and Priscilla Bell, who were the only children
admitted.   At this sight I was so happy as to be present.
You may be sure I was not a little anxious on account of
my girl, who very unexpectedly remembered all instructions, but kissed the Queen's hand with such a grace that
I thought the Princess Dowager would have smothered
her with kisses; and on her return to the drawing-room,
such a report was made of her to his Majesty, that Miss
was sent for again, when she was so lucky as to afford
the King great amusement, in particular by telling him
she loved the King, though she must not love fine
things; and that her grandpapa would not allow her to
make a courtesy.   The simplicity of her dress and

manner seemed to give great pleasure ; and she was
dismissed with as great applause as my most boundless
wishes could desire. Her sweet face made such an
impression on the Duke of York, that I rejoiced she was
only five instead of fifteen.

" The King, you may observe, never sat down, nor did
he taste anything during the whole time. Her Majesty
drank tea, which was brought her on a silver waiter by
brother John, who delivered it to the lady-in-waiting,
and she presented it kneeling, which to us, who had
never seen that ceremony before, appeared as pretty as
any of the parade. The rest of the royal family and
nobility repaired to the place prepared for refreshments.
Our kitchen upon this occasion was turned into a tea-
room, and coffee and chocolate were prepared for above
a hundred people, and four females to attend; besides,
there was a cold collation of hams, fowls, tongues, hung
beef, &c., all served in small plates, for this repast was
only designed for a bit by way of staying the stomach.
The dressers, after being covered with a fine cloth, were
spread with white biscuits, rusks, &c. Through fatigue,
mamma was very soon obliged to retire; then sister
Weston was declared mistress of the ceremony, and
sister Patty her attendant; as for us, we were so happy
as to have nothing to do but to converse with the ladies,
some of whom were very sociable.

" As they staid till seven, the drawing-room and
balcony were illuminated, which added prodigiously to
the beauty of the scene. But what charmed us most

of all, was their Majesties being left with us by themselves, having sent all away before them, except the two
ladies in waiting on the queen; and, indeed, this has
been deemed by the public the greatest mark of respect
they could bestow, to trust themselves without so much
as a guard in the house, or any of the nobles. The
leave they took of us was such as we might expect from
our equals; full of apologies for the trouble they had
given us, and returning thanks for the entertainment;
which they were so careful to have fully explained, that
the Queen came up to us as we were all standing on one
side the door, and had every word interpreted, and left
us in astonishment at her condescension, my brothers
attending them to the coach in the same manner they
had received them, only with the additional honour of
assisting the Queen to get in. In short, they omitted
nothing that could demonstrate respect ; an instance of
which the King gave, by ordering twenty-four of the
life guards, who were drawn up, during his Majesty's
stay, in Bow Church-Yard, to be placed opposite our
house all night, lest any of the canopy should be pulled
down by the mob, in which there were one hundred
yards of silk damask."

In this unaffected natural description of the scene, the
queen, it will be seen, is the central figure; and it
furnishes a very pleasing idea of the fashion in which
her simple and even engaging manners affected the
spectators.

She began at once to distinguish herself as a person of

marked character, and—what was astonishing in one so young—as an admirable manager of a household. It must be said, indeed, that this seemed in a manner to be her special taste and occupation. She cared little for amusements. She had a German's fondness for dancing, she liked her game of cards, and for music she had a passion ; but her real enjoyment and pastime was found in the household, and in the small dramatic incidents that arose from the mixture of dependants of all classes— ladies-in-waiting, " dressers," grooms of the chambers—all German and English. Expenses she regulated strictly, and, later, there were stories circulated of mean savings and " cheeseparings," for which there was little or no foundation. It was well known there could not be a more liberal and generous pair in their presents and charities, but waste and imposition and lack of control were odious to them.

The new queen had brought with her from Mecklenburg two faithful attendants who are well known to us, and in one at least of whom we have a strong interest. These were Mrs. Haggerdorn and Mrs. or Madam Schwellenberg. Who that loves humour and high comedy of dramatic character does not know " the Schwellenberg " who, odiously as she is represented in Miss Burney's lively pages, was really a very honest, faithful and worthy woman. Both were destined to remain with the queen for many years. Mrs. Schwellenberg is said to have been " extremely courteous in her manner, much respected by all the domestics, and devotedly attached to the royal

family, who entertained for her the sincerest affection.
She has been held up to ridicule by a profligate wit as
a person of sordid disposition." This was Dr. Walcot.

Besides these there had been allotted to her Majesty
as "dressers," an Englishwoman, Miss Laverock, and
Miss Pascal, a German, who was sent from the princess
dowager's household, with the view, as the young queen
suspected, of being a spy upon her. She therefore never
liked her or encouraged her—which treatment Miss Pascal
accepted with good humour, for she was a cheerful, clever
person, and pursued her business as though she was
thoroughly acceptable. This was but the beginning of
the many household or servant intrigues which were
later to rage. Miss Pascal later became Mrs. Thielke.[1]

One of her maids of honour was, strange to say, the
celebrated, or perhaps, notorious, Miss Chudleigh, who
was presently to invite the attention of the whole kingdom and become the heroine of a scandalous bigamy case.
It will be seen that the selection of the queen's ladies had
not been made very judiciously. Two, at least, the
flighty Duchess of Hamilton and Miss Chudleigh,
certainly lacked good sense. Some of the other ladies,
as we shall see later, distinguished themselves by
escapades, elopements, etc. Miss Chudleigh about this
time entertained her royal mistress with an odd entertainment thus sketched by Mr. Walpole :—

[1] Not long ago, surveying the quaint old church at Kew, so associated
with the queen and so many a sad and painful scene, a headstone caught
my eye which was " sacred to the memory " of this very Mrs. Thielke.

"Oh, that you had been at her ball the other night !
History could never describe it, and keep its countenance.
The Queen's real birth-day, you know, is not kept : this
maid of honour kept it—nay, while the court is in
mourning, expected people to be out of mourning : the
Queen's family really was so ; Lady Northumberland
having desired leave for them. A scaffold was erected
in Hyde Park for fire-works. To show the illuminations
without to more advantage, the company were received
in an apartment totally dark, where they remained for
two hours. The fire-works were fine, and succeeded well.
On each side of the court were two large scaffolds for
the virgin's tradespeople. When the fire-works ceased,
a large scene was lighted in the court, representing their
Majesties, on each side of which were six obelisks,
painted with emblems, and illuminated ; mottoes
beneath in Latin and English. First, for the Prince of
Wales, a ship, *Multorum Spes*. Second, for the Princess
Dowager, a bird of Paradise, and two little ones, *Meos
ad sidera tollo*. Third, Duke of York, a temple, *Virtuti
et honori*. Fourth, Princess Augusta, a bird of Paradise,
Non habet parem. Fifth, the three younger princes, an
orange tree, *Promittat et dat*. Sixth, the two younger
princesses, the flower crown imperial. I forget the Latin ;
the translation was silly enough, ' Bashful in youth,
graceful in age.' The lady of the house made many
apologies for the poorness of the performance, which she
said was only oil-paper, painted by one of her servants ;
but it really was fine and pretty. Behind the house was

a cenotaph for the Princess Elizabeth, a kind of illuminated cradle : the motto, ' All the honours the dead can
receive.' This burying ground was a strange codicil to a
festival ; and what was still more strange, about one in
the morning this sarcophagus burst out into crackers
and guns. The Margrave of Anspach began the ball with
the virgin. The supper was most sumptuous." [1]

Another of the queen's maids of honour was Miss
Vernon, who became indirectly associated with a
strange story. Her *femme de chambre* was a girl named
Sarah Wilson, who broke open one of the royal cabinets,
which she rifled of some valuable jewels. She was
detected, tried, and sentenced to death. By the humane
interposition of the queen she was " pardoned," as it
was called—that is, sent to Maryland and sold as a slave
to one Mr. Devall. She, however, contrived to escape,

---

[1] As all the proceedings of this extraordinary lady had something
grotesque or odd, we find Mason, the poet, writing to Lord Harcourt,
that at court in 1759 she stooped down to try and pick up a piece of
dirty paper ; but it was noticed could not succeed in stooping sufficiently
owing to her stoutness. A certain doctor, who saw her difficulty,
attempted to pick it up, but he also proved too fat, and could get no
lower than his knees, to the general hilarity of the pages and officers
on guard.

It was not till the year 1775 that Buckingham House was settled
on the queen as her dower house ; a committee of the House of
Commons resolving that it should be so settled in lieu of Somerset
House, and that after her demise it should revert to the Crown. The
palace of Somerset House, which had been originally settled on her,
was taken back again, "for the purpose of erecting and establishing
certain public offices." Hence Sir W. Chambers' stately pile, which is
one of the few classical buildings of the metropolis, but which the
embankment has robbed of much of its effect as a riverside palace.

and found her way to Charlestown. She then gave out that she was sister of the Queen of England, the Princess Susanna Caroline Matilda, and the clothes she wore, with some of the stolen ornaments, seemed to support her story. She had fled, she said, to avoid a hateful marriage. This tale imposed on many, and as she had picked up stories of the court and could tell much about the king and queen, she was received into many families and treated with profound respect. Some she admitted to the honour of kissing her hand. She of course levied contributions, which were to be repaid many fold when she " got her rights." Suspicions, however, were presently aroused, and her former master, hearing of her doings, had her arrested and brought back.

Miss Vernon's mother, Lady Harriet, was one of Princess Amelia's ladies ; her other daughter, Lady Grosvenor, figured in a notorious scandal. Miss Vernon herself later became the heroine of a wild adventure.

But a sort of ill-luck seemed to pursue the early house-hold appointments of the new queen. Lord Pembroke, one of her suite, was married to a lovely woman, whom he abruptly deserted, resigning all his appointments at the court and in the army to fly to the continent with a young girl.[1] The failure of these selections was not

---

[1] The deserted lady survived till the year 1831, when she died at the age of 93. The odd eccentric humours of the fashionable folk were well illustrated by one of the freaks of the Duchess of Grafton, who had been divorced and remarried about the same time. On the day before the divorce she wrote letters signed " Anne Grafton ; " on the day after,

owing to the queen, they had been made for her. When she came to have a free hand, nothing could be better than her choice.

Before the visit to the city, just described, the king, on the meeting of Parliament, took occasion to pay a public compliment to his bride, who he declared was "eminently distinguished by every virtue and amiable endowment," and afforded him "all possible domestic enjoyment." He appealed to the House, in his "affectionate regard for her," to make a suitable provision for her. The Commons responded with alacrity, and the handsome jointure of £100,000 a year with two palaces were settled upon her. A further provision, the usual one of £100,000 a year, was made for her in case of the king's demise. The place of residence, or jointure house, had been the old Somerset House, not yet replaced by Chambers' handsome structure. At the end of the Mall there stood a fine old brick mansion which had been built by Sheffield, Duke of Buckingham, in 1703. It was of the style and character of Marlborough House, and was joined by semicircular colonnades to two pavilions. This the king purchased for the moderate sum of £21,000, and fitted up as a dower house for the queen. It henceforth becomes very familiar to us through the reign as "The Queen's House," and many interesting transactions occurred there. When the regent came to the throne, growing tired of Carlton House, he levelled the Queen's House and erected others signed "Anne Liddell," her maiden name; and on the next day, others signed "Anne Ossory," her new one.

a substantial portion of the present Buckingham Palace. About this time also the house at Kew was purchased which had belonged to a private gentleman—Mr. G. Molyneux—who had been secretary to George II. when Prince of Wales. Here were beautiful gardens, 120 acres in extent ; while additions and improvements were made by Kent the architect. At Kew, much that was dramatic as well as disastrous was to occur. Further on there was the old palace at Richmond, then habitable, to which the royal family, always fond of changing residence, used occasionally to repair. The old Somerset House before the end of the year was handed over to the State, and Sir C. Sheffield was employed to alter Buckingham House. An additional wing was added on the garden side, and on that facing Pimlico " a most elegant building for a library." This was to be the royal family's town palace ; but all " Public Days " and Festas were to be held at St. James's Palace, close by. By June, 1763, the alterations had been completed and the royal pair "moved in." On the occasion they gave a regular house-warming, when " a most elegant entertainment was planned," a concert, a ball, the garden to be illuminated, all under the direction of a German, Mr. Kuffe.

At this time indeed, as was to be expected, there was a perfect round of gaieties. Parties were regularly given at St. James's Palace twice a week, when two and three hundred guests were invited. The music was a marked feature, the king's private band performing,

Stanley was at the organ, and Cramer, the king's master, at the piano.   Crosdill was the violoncellist, and Miss Linley, it was said, sang.   The queen declared her intention of visiting the theatres once a week, and would select her own plays.   There may have been a humorous apropos in her earliest choice, " Rule a wife, and have a wife." We may assume that the plot and dialogue must have been explained to her beforehand.   The rough Lady Townshend, whose " good things " were being circulated, on hearing that Lady Northumberland had been appointed a lady of the bedchamber, declared that it was quite proper, for as the queen knew no English, that lady would teach her the vulgar tongue.

CHAPTER IV.

UNFORTUNATELY, at this opening of her course, there can be little doubt that the life of the young queen was scarcely a happy one. The king was worried with ministerial troubles, and the princess dowager, secure in the support of the favourite Lord Bute, was able to exert all the influence and authority which age and knowledge of the world and the position of a parent would give her over a young and inexperienced couple. The young queen was unable to resist. The creatures of the princess-mother were placed about her, and it was even said that a regular " spy," Miss Dashwood, a beauty of the last reign, was appointed to report to her mother-in-law. A sort of palace despotism controlled all her actions. The king himself, strongly under his mother's influence, was not inclined to interfere, and assumed that all was done rightly. Already she was not allowed to be too intimate with the English ladies of her household. It was laid down as being formal etiquette of the court that they should not approach her save under the direction of the German attendants. Card-playing, which she loved, was presently interdicted.

Naturally, too, there were the German and the English factions of dependents; each jealously contending for their royal mistress's favour. This rivalry led to very unbecoming contentions, in which her authority suffered ; for we find with surprise the common menials and persons scarcely above them arrogantly dictating the terms and conditions of their service, and threatening to go back to Germany unless particular privileges were given them. The poor queen had about as much anxiety and trouble with her dependents as her husband had with his insubordinate ministers or servants.

"The Schwellenberg," who is described as a very shrewd, ambitious woman, and much more capable and active at this time than at the period when we know her so well in Miss Burney's animated pages, when she was borne down with infirmities, now began to take her line at once. She claimed to be called " Madame," to distinguish her from her compatriot Haggerdorn.   She fixed that her rooms should be next the queen's, so that no one should gain admittance without first obtaining her "permit."   Naturally, people began to complain and grumble at this assumed despotism, and many thus hindered in their approaches took offence. The queen could not afford to lose her two compatriots, and they knew their hold upon her. Gradually the aggressive lady came to be the head of the wardrobe, and was placed, or placed herself, over all the persons employed.

The expenditure then was growing great, for the dresses ordered in profusion were changed every three months, so the severest control and discipline were necessary and duly exercised. The influence of this masterful woman increased daily; by-and-by she no longer dressed the queen, but looked on and directed. Everyone that wanted anything had to propitiate her or ask through her. Thus Nicholay, one of the pages, actually got his four sons provided for, all through the Schwellenberg's agency, while the Papendieck, who had been drawn from Germany by great promises, but did not enjoy her favour, could obtain nothing. Complaints of wranglings soon reached the king, who required that she should be dismissed and sent home. The queen, we are told, was distressed, not so much at losing her best friend, as at the unpleasantness and annoyance which a change would bring about. She interceded with her husband in the presence of the princess dowager his mother, and was told that her lady might remain, but must alter her behaviour. She must not be preferred to others, and not influence the queen. This rough censure, given before one who would have enjoyed it, deeply hurt the young queen. All this business, indeed, it was believed, was got up by the princess dowager, who continued cold and distant to her daughter-in-law.

In due time it was known that the birth of a child was imminent, and on the morning of August 12th, 1762, hurried messengers were speeding to summon the various personages who were entitled to be present

The princess dowager, all the ladies of the court and great officers of State were summoned, but the Archbishop of Canterbury alone was admitted into the royal chamber. Her ladies were obliged to remain in another room, the door being left open. At a little after seven the birth took place, and the future Prince of Wales, regent and king, whose erratic course was to bring such trouble and anxieties to his family and to the nation, came into the world. The king presented the messenger who brought him the joyful news with £500.[1] Thus the course of good fortune which had attended the new queen was uninterrupted, and the nation was at once gratified.

It might be imagined that this auspicious event might have led to some relaxation of her captivity, but the *cordon* round her was too strong, and not for some years was her own natural force of character able to assert itself. Of what sort this *cordon* was we shall presently see.

When Princess Elizabeth was born, May 22nd, 1770, there were some birthday festivities in progress, which the queen could not of course attend. But she sent some birthday verses in honour of the occasion—written from her bed—in pencil. They are not without merit according to the standard of to-day.

---

[1] It was noticed that the queen, departing from the old routine of being assisted by one of her own sex, availed herself of Mr. Hunter's aid. Later, on such occasions there were always crowds of applications for the office of nurse. Once, in 1779, "a female elegantly dressed in blue and silver" was introduced into her Majesty's bedroom, who looked at her from head to foot, and dismissed her with the remark, "Your appearance is that of a queen, and not of a nurse!"

I.

When monarchs give a grace to fate,
    And rise as princes shou'd,
Less highly born, than truly great,
    Less dignified, than good :

II.

What joy the natal day can bring,
    From whence our hopes began,
Which gave the nation such a king,
    And being, such a man !

III.

The sacred source of endless pow'r,
    Delighted sees him born,
And kindly marks the circling hour,
    That spoke him into morn.

IV.

Beholds him with the kindest eye
    Which goodness can bestow ;
And shows a brighter crown on high
    Than e'er he wore below.

There was a good old custom in the house of Hanover
of giving their daughters family names : just as Frederick
and William belong to the royal house of Prussia. Such
were Augusta, Sophia, Amelia, Elizabeth, etc. These
good old names have a character, and when her
present gracious Majesty was being christened, the
regent, who often displayed a sense of propriety in
matters of etiquette, reminded his brothers of this custom,
and made a sort of protest against the names chosen—
Victoria Alexandrina—but without effect. For there
were reasons of *la haute politique.*

The queen, as is known, was destined in the course of years to furnish the nation with one of the largest royal families on record, having had no less than fifteen children.[1] Of these, Princess Mary, who was married to the Duke of Gloucester, her cousin, was the longest lived, and survived till the year 1857. What strange far-off scenes could she reveal, even to the dreadful episodes at Kew which she witnessed as a child !   The Duchess of Cambridge survived even longer, dying some ten years ago aged ninety-one.

The servant trouble now began to grow more acute, mainly owing to the intrigues of the princess's retainers. There was no authority to control the two, or rather the three parties. The poor queen seemed helpless. Her own faithful attendants whom she had brought from Germany were discontented and wished to go home.

[1] This royal roll is as follows :—

George Augustus Frederick, Prince of Wales, b. 1762 ; d. 1830.

Frederick, Duke of York, b. 1763 ; d. 1827.

William, b. 1765 ; d. 1837.

Edward, Duke of Kent, b. 1767 ; d. 1820.

Ernest Augustus, Duke of Cumberland, b. 1771 ; d. 1851.

Augustus Frederick, Duke of Sussex, b. 1773 ; d. 1843.

Adolphus Frederick, Duke of Cambridge, b. 1774 ; d. 1850.

Octavius, b. Feb. 1779 ; d. 1783.

Alfred, b. Sept. 1780 ; d. Aug. 1782.

Charlotte Augusta Matilda, b. 1766 ; m. 18th May, 1797, Frederick, then Duke, later King, of Wurtemburg, d. Oct. 1828.

Augusta Sophia, b. Nov. 1768 ; d. 1840.

Elizabeth, b. May, 1770 ; m. 1818 ; he d. 1829 ; she d. 1840.

Mary, b. 1776; m. Duke of Gloucester, 1816 ; d. 1857.

Sophia, b. 1777 ; d. 1848.

Amelia, b. 1783 ; d. 1810.

They resented, too, the economies which were being made in the royal establishment. But now their young mistress was beginning to show a certain independence and intention to take matters into her own hands. One Albert, whom she had induced to leave Mecklenburg with her under great promises, was in revolt, and it is strange to read the plain, free terms in which he vented his grievances. He begged to be allowed to go away either on pension or with some appointment in the house of the reigning duke. The queen refused, on which he reminded her very plainly of all her promises which had induced him to quit his country, of her suggestion that he should marry, his own rooted objections to going with her, and her assurance that she would always be his friend. He claimed that he had done his part. The queen acknowledged all this, lamented a certain groom incident, but said she could not interfere, as the king had shown no disapprobation of the matter. She then told him that as it was necessary to be most economical in their civil list, all " perquisites " would be less, and for the future persons would be taken into their service " whom they could more generally employ ; " that they were compelled to suffer privations themselves, and would be obliged to make some others, which those who had hitherto been in every way considered and had lived like gentlemen would, she feared, feel also. The dependent then spoke of his daughter who was growing up, saying that he hoped she would be provided for about the princesses,

and that he had been training her up for the purpose.
The queen replied that instead of keeping their own
people and conferring favours as before, they felt it more
suitable to have strangers. " Less was expected—much
more generally done. Fatal mistake ! " On this Albert
adds from *his* point of view : " The new appointments
felt no interest, neither duty nor respect ; and as to
fidelity, such was not understood."

Early in the year 1764 Princess Augusta, one of the
king's sisters, was married to the Prince of Brunswick
Lunenberg—an alliance in every way unsuitable, like
that of another sister, the ill-fated Caroline Matilda, which
was soon to follow. No one there dreamed that the
future daughter of the Brunswick pair was to become the
wife of the child so recently born—the baby Prince of
Wales, and to come to the throne—nor did the family
anticipate the sore trials that were in store for them, the
loss of dominions, the death of husband and son on the
field of battle.

The court fancied " the Brunswicks " were hunting for
popularity, and there were many stories of the coldness
with which the guests were treated. The mob continued to follow the pair, and at theatres and other
public places greeted them with hurrahs. It was suspected
they were intriguing against the court. It was said that
almost the first question put to them on their arrival
was, " *When do you go ?* " Even the Royal servants were
forbidden to wear their new liveries, and there was no
salute of guns. When the young king and queen

went to the play they were received in silence. The crowd suspected what was going on.

The Duchess of Brunswick long remembered this unhandsome treatment. Thirty years later when Lord Malmesbury was at Brunswick, she opened herself to him freely—abused her Majesty heartily—said she was an envious, intriguing spirit—told anecdotes of her first coming over from Strelitz—accused her of disliking her mother (the Princess of Wales) and herself: she was quite jealous of both. She had even seized the opportunity, when the princess was dying, of altering the rank of her ladies of the bedchamber, all which was prejudiced exaggeration—not unnatural, however; but the truth is, it was only after all the precedents of human nature and party feeling that she should fancy that the person she disliked should have the same feeling to her.

It is amusing to read that, among other household difficulties, their Majesties in 1775 had to encounter a sort of strike among the maids of honour! These young ladies were entitled to their supper every evening at the royal charges, but being generally absent, owing to their duties at the palace or elsewhere, they were seldom able to partake of it. They accordingly met and drew up a petition requesting that some pecuniary compensation should be made to them. The good-natured king went into the matter, and decided that the ladies should each have seventy pounds a year additional salary.

The royal family of England has always been noted for

its collections of costly jewels.   Queen Charlotte's famous
set of pearls were held to be the finest in Europe, and
were valued at £150,000.   They remained in the possession of her present Majesty for twenty years, until the
year 1857, when they were handed over to King George
of Hanover, as Queen Charlotte had left them by will to
her son Ernest, the Duke of Cumberland.   Mr. Greville
seems to say—but the passage is not very clear—that on
her death the regent had appropriated all jewels and
other property—so he was told by the Duke of York.
One of the present Queen's Jubilee presents was a
superb set of emeralds, worth, it is said, £20,000.   This
came from the Czar and Czarina.

Her mother's request on parting was that the queen
should not receive the sacrament when wearing her
jewels, and she obtained the king's leave not to do so—
though he desired that she should.   One of the court
tale-bearers brought this to the princess dowager, who
went to her and insisted that the jewels should be worn ;
and in spite of her tears, so it was done.

Long after she told Miss Burney how well she had
liked at first her jewels and ornaments as queen.   " But
how soon," she said, " was that over !   Believe me, Miss
Burney, it is the pleasure of a week—a fortnight at most
—and to return no more.   I thought at first I should
always choose to wear them ; but the fatigue and trouble
of putting them on, and the care they required, and the
fear of losing them, believe me, ma'am, in a fortnight's
time I longed again for my own earlier dress."

In the same conversation she recalled her youth, describing how she had never cared for dress, or for anything beyond neatness and comfort, and though but seventeen when she became a queen, it was only her eyes that were dazzled, not her mind, and the delusion speedily vanished.

At the court balls ladies were seen wearing £50,000 worth. The court jewellers did an immense business, notably Cox, of Shoe Lane, who was having "constant interviews with their Majesties." It was noticed, however, that the queen never assumed her ornaments save when the king took part in the ceremonial. She always appeared attired with much simplicity, but becomingly.

As her Majesty, and the king also, were so fond of jewellery, they must have been much pleased by a very acceptable present which arrived from India in 1769. A Bengal Nabob sent over a box containing a great number of diamonds—"a bulse" it was called—and other rich jewellery, which were intended for the king, who presented the queen with the greatest portion. This "bulse," moreover, excited much discussion and many allusions in the House of Commons and elsewhere, it being supposed to have some connection with the reported spoliation of the natives in India which later led to the famous prosecution of Hastings.

We constantly hear of daring robberies and attempts at robberies even in the royal presence. At one of the Drawing Rooms Lord Mexborough had his star—one of special value and magnificence—cut from his ribbon. At another Sir G. Warren lost his diamond star of the Bath.

There were stories of jewels dropped and picked up by persons of position who never restored them. On one occasion at court her Majesty dropped one of her ear-rings, and diligent search was made for it. A foreign nobleman was seen to stoop and pick up something, but declared that it was his own sleeve button.

On the birthday festival in 1769 the queen's diamonds seem to have surprised everybody; many of them the courtiers had seen, but she had so many additional ones and of so extraordinary a size that the princes said the description sounded like a fairy tale. She wore some of those in her head that the Nabob sent the king as a present, and for which his Majesty had returned a lion. She had another of a surprising magnitude which was placed on a nosegay of jewels. She said their weight was a great fatigue. Some daring attempts at robbery were made at the first court ball after the marriage of the Duke of York in 1792. As the Prince of Wales was talking to the king, he felt a tug at his sword, and looking down found that the diamond guard had been broken off and hung suspended by a small piece of wire. The precious stones of the guard were said to be worth £3000. A fashionably dressed man was standing close by who was supposed to have been the author of the attempt.

Indeed everything at court seemed to be conducted in a highly *degagé* style, and the sovereign was treated in rather familiar fashion. When in 1768 the king's sister, the Queen of Denmark, was confined, an express arrived in London to the Danish Ambassador, who immediately communicated the joyful news to Lord Weymouth, the minister. The latter was going to the king on business, and, incredible as it may seem, actually forgot to mention this important matter. By-and-by, at some court or levee, this Danish envoy came up to his Majesty, expecting, no doubt, a compliment on his promptness. To his surprise the king never mentioned the topic, and talked of everything else. At last the minister wished him joy, to more surprise on the king's side. An amusing scene.

The same carelesness was shown in attending the royal pair. So early in the reign as 1766 the king and queen were driving at Richmond in an open chaise, when they were insulted by a man and a woman, who cursed them—and the woman threw a shoe at the queen. They were immediately seized, and it was curiously stated that " by the laws of the country they might be put to death " —but it was thought that the thing would not be noticed.

The picturesque Kew Green, with its surrounding houses and gardens, to this hour preserves a sort of quaint, old-fashioned tone. About it lingers a faint flavour of the old royal days, when it enjoyed the favour of the court. When the royal children were being brought up there, there was a colony established of the numerous person-ages who were entrusted with their education. Lady Charlotte Finch lived in a house in the gardens—close to the river—these gardens not yet being in possession of the nation. Miss Planta, the English teacher, lived in the palace.[1]

Bishop Hurd, who at this time was preceptor of the elder boys, had a house on the green. And here were the two surgeons, Pringle and Hawkins. Dr. Majendie also lived at Kew, and Bishop Newton. There are some substantial red brick houses close to the present railings of the gardens, which were occupied by the young princes. Many of the retainers and some of the suite were lodged on the other side of the river.

On fashionable days vast crowds of the nobility and others drove down, and the green was covered with equipages, and it was stated that often as much as £300 was taken at the bridge toll-house, which seems an exaggeration.

When the family were approaching Kew the natives would show their attachment by assembling in force on the green to welcome them, drawn up in lines along the road, and arrayed in their " Sunday clothes." There was a band, and loud hurrahs. The good queen said warmly, " I shall always love *little Kew* for this." It was remarked that she could dismiss her ladies without any tone of authority, but would always use some such

[1] For those who enjoy Miss Burney's lively chronicles it is always curious and interesting to meet with persons bearing the old names of their personages. I myself have met a Mr. Planta who was of the governess's family, and for many years regularly paid an annuity to a descendant of Miss Burney's sister. We also now hear of Goldsworthys and others.

gracious form as, " Now I will let you go ; or on occasion Schwellenberg might say in her odd English, " When
you have done *from the queen*, come to my room."

On feast days, birthdays, and such occasions, trifling
presents, according to the German fashion, were inter-
changed and expected. With a native simplicity, the
princesses showed what they had received with great
enjoyment. There were whisperings and mystery as to
the present from mamma. They took the form of *etwees*,
purses and the like. The queen often gave her ladies
handsome gowns when they were attending her on some
visit of state.

In the matter of improving and altering their many
palaces, the royal family showed great energy and
enterprise. At one time they were anxious to repair
and inhabit the picturesque old building at Richmond,
and attempted some negotiations with the local
authorities for purchasing additional land. These
approaches, however, were not favourably received, and
the king and queen turned their thoughts to the
improvement of Windsor and Kew. The Richmond
folk then saw their mistake and consented to give the
ground, but it was too late.[1]

Lady Mary Coke supplies some lively sketches of the
court life at this time. The queen, she tells us, wore an

---

[1] Richmond even now retains much of its court tone and flavour. The
striking " Maid of Honour Row " still stands, the fragment of the
palace has been well restored, and is inhabited, but the old theatre and
manager's house is levelled.

English nightgown, and ordered Lady Charlotte Finch
to do the same. She looked sharply after all the ladies,
and was very strict in etiquette and ceremonial. She
would come rather late to prayers at St. George's Chapel,
and would be extra vigilant as to the attendance of
others. On one occasion when she complained that she
did not see Lady Mary there, the latter in her lively way
said, " I am sure I made my curtsey as soon as I rose
from my knees. I could not get up during the Lord's
Prayer."

The good fortune of the queen was not without its
effect in attracting numbers of her family to London, and
in about a year or two after the marriage we find two of
her Majesty's brothers enjoying all the pleasures of the
metropolis. A house was taken for one in Pall Mall at
the queen's expense, who was eager in her inquiries after
all her old friends, Madame de Grabow, Pastor Gensner,
and the rest. She was not so pleased when there
arrived from Strelitz, in the following year, 1764, a
grotesque countess, one Mme. de Yerbsen, whose appearance and behaviour excited the ridicule of the courtiers.
It was reported that she had once boxed the King of
Prussia's ears ! The queen was rather ashamed of her
compatriot, but her remark was quoted as clever : " This
is not the sort of dress we have at Strelitz; this lady
always dresses herself as capriciously there as your
Duchess of Queensberry does here."

Her rather impoverished family by-and-by gave
trouble to their great connection. The queen's brothers,

as we have seen, continued to pay visits to London; the head of the family was seriously embarrassed. His debts, owing to these excursions, were said to reach thirty thousand pounds, and the good-natured queen had often to assist her impecunious relatives out of her own pocket. When Lord Halifax died we are told that she exerted her influence to get Lord Suffolk appointed in his place. This nobleman had taken interest in her family and engaged to arrange their embarrassed affairs, which he did. One of the family, Prince Ernest, became attached to a very wealthy heiress, and was eager to marry, but the royal family had objections, and the plan came to nothing.

But the wise queen took care, on the whole, not to furnish ground for any charges of undue " nepotism," though she did not neglect her relatives. Any distinctions they received were of an honorary kind. The Duke of Mecklenburg was thus made a Knight of the Garter, his brother Charles became governor of the little town of Zell, and Prince George, after waiting long in England, received a commission in the Hanoverian army. But in her private capacity she was always generous to them, making them handsome presents.

Large as was the king's family and many as were the alliances to be made by his sisters and brothers and his own numerous children it was a strange thing that so few of them turned out well or could be considered prosperous. Some careers were absolutely of the most disastrous kind, and brought disaster to those with whom they were connected.

Thus, the marriage of the king's sister, Caroline Augusta, to the King of Denmark took place under the fairest auspices, and the alliance was considered " a good match," as it is called. But for the interposition of the king her brother, the unfortunate lady would have fared ill, and perhaps lost her life. Some frigates were despatched to carry her away, and she was allowed to choose a retreat at Zell in Hanover. Her story is certainly one of the most romantic and interesting kind, and though Sir M. Wraxall and others have given minute accounts of the affair, the mystery has never been wholly cleared up. There were many schemes for her release or rescue, which she did not live long enough to profit by, for she died on May 10th, 1775, of a malignant fever, after an illness of five days. Her strange husband had been recently in London, exciting much attention by his capricious doings.

Meanwhile the king was harassed and worried by political difficulties. Ministers, politicians and the revolutionary "patriots" joined to make his life a burden. The ministers, presuming on his youth, treated him with an insolent dictation. Wilkes was displaying his almost ferocious hostility, while the princess-mother and her favourite were exciting public odium. It was not surprising that in 1765 the harassed young monarch became seriously ill. The nature of this illness was carefully concealed. His ministers, when he was recovering, found his manner " a good deal estranged." But the truth leaked out that it was a light form of the mental disorder that afflicted him some twenty years later.

He was seized with a feverish attack, with " a humour

on his breast," and had to be blooded four times. He however recovered, and the incident showed in what a perilous position the sovereignty was : for in the case of his demise, no provision had been made for providing for carrying on the government. The real and secret alarm was, that it would fall to the ambitious princess-mother and her creature, Lord Bute. A Regency Bill was at once brought forward, which, owing to the struggles and jealousies of the factions, underwent the most singular changes before it could be passed. The king's object was to secure all power for the queen at first. All the five princes were put aside. The regency was to be *in petto*, with four secret nominations. Then, as jealousies arose, the princes were introduced into the Bill and the queen was named as Regent. Awkward questions were then raised as to whether the queen had been naturalized, and how was even the term Royal Family to be defined. It was finally carried that the Princess Dowager should be excluded altogether, a great affront to one who was the queen's mother. The queen was named Regent and the matter finally settled.

During this crisis the princess and Lord Bute tried to keep from the queen the knowledge that the king's mind was affected, and to keep her from his side. The queen herself became seriously ill from anxiety and trouble, but deeply resented the treatment she had met with from her mother-in-law. On his recovery the king returned to her and was hers more than ever.

Under this treatment it was natural that the queen's spirits sank, and at the play it was remarked how dejected

and melancholy she was.   There were even tears in her
eyes, and she complained that when one of the princesses
was to be married they told her nothing about it or
when it was to be.   She was eager that her favourite,
Colonel Graeme, should be made vice-admiral of Scotland.   But the Duke of Grafton bluntly refused, which
deeply offended her.

The royal birthdays were always kept with solemnities
which must have been fatiguing and oppressive.   The
queen had to endure a congratulatory oration from the
Archbishop of Canterbury, and then hold a long Drawing
Room.   This was followed by the inevitable " Birthday
Ode," performed by the full strength of a royal band
and chorus.   It was not surprising that the queen broke
down under the strain, and had to terminate the
ceremonies without receiving all her guests.

Birthday odes are now happily things of the past, and
must have been an intolerable burden for the inspired
writer as well as for the persons who were thus complimented.   The laureate was annually called upon
to supply his regular article ; he found the verse, and
Dr. Boys the music, while the royal victims had to
sit patiently and listen for an hour or so to the strophes,
antistrophes, recitatives, &c.   Thus Mr. William White-
head, the laureate :—

> " The *genuine offspring* of the Brunswick name
> Proved his high birth's hereditary name,
> And the applauding nation hailed with joy
> Their future hero in the ' intrepid boy.'

" The *genuine* offspring " is decidedly good; so is the
proving the high birth of an hereditary name; also the
hailing for joy, and the " intrepid boy."

In the earlier days of the reign, these birthday
celebrations were carried out on a very magnificent scale,
and at great cost.   In 1763, for instance, a superb temple
and bridge were erected in the gardens of Buckingham
House, with some 4000 coloured lamps ; also paintings,
transparencies, depicting the glories of the country.   A
grand orchestra, as it was then thought, of fifty of " the
most eminent performers," played in front of the temple.
This was a surprise for his Majesty, who knew nothing
of what was intended—the preparations being all com·
pleted within a couple of days.   On the night in
question, the queen suddenly threw open the shutters
of the windows and revealed the dazzling show to her
astonished husband.   In addition to the laureate's effort,
her Majesty, always fond of composition, indited songs.
At the queen's illumination at Kew was a large transparent picture, under which were the following lines,
written by her Majesty :—

> " Our prayers are heard and Providence restores
> A patriot King to bless Britannia's shores ;
> *But not to Britain is the bliss confin'd,*
> All Europe hails the friend of human kind.
> If such the general joy, what words can show
> The change to transport, from the depths of woe,
> In those permitted to embrace again
> The best of fathers, husbands, and of men !"

Personal addresses and epilogues have long since

vanished. But Miss Brunton might have been proud
to come forward at the end of "The Dramatist" and
deliver these "apposite lines," their Majesties listening :--

"Ah, Floriville, if you would have pure unsullied love, never travel
out of this country—depend on't,

> "'No foreign climes such high examples prove
> Of wedded pleasure—of connubial love,
> Long in this isle domestic joys have grown
> Nursed in the cottage—*cherished on the throne!*'"

When the attempt on the king's life was made at
Drury Lane, it has been often told how the adroit
Sheridan fashioned an impromptu verse for "God Save
the King," though Mr. Burgess has been also credited
with this feat. When Princess Amelia recovered from a
serious attack, the event was celebrated by a fête at
Frogmore, the decorations of which were designed by
Princess Elizabeth, the artist of the royal family. It is
evidence of the pleasant, unsophisticated relations of the
king with his subjects, that after the banquet those free-
and-easy performers, but privileged favourites, Elliston,
Quick, and Mrs. Mattocks, were introduced, who delivered some apropos lines written by Lady Sudley.

The good and sensible queen was careful to patronize
English wares, and in 1769, as we have seen, she announced
that she would always wear an English nightgown, and
required Lady C. Finch to do the same. "The king likes
it." Formerly no lady could appear before her in a white
apron, but this was now tolerated. At one Drawing

Room an incident occurred which caused much talk. Lady Egmont brought a lady to be presented, who wore a bride's dress, and as Lady Northampton, her daughter, had lately been married, every one thought that this was the new Lady Northampton. The lady-in-waiting brought her forward as such, and the queen with smiling cordiality welcomed her with the customary salute. It turned out that it was only a Mrs. Hulst.

Nowadays when we see the palaces and their approaches strongly guarded by police and soldiers, whom it is impossible to pass without the *consigne*, it seems strange to look back to the almost patriarchal familiarity which obtained between the royal family and their subjects. The police protection of the royal dwellings was of the most indifferent kind, with the result that we hear of constant intrusions and invasions by mad persons and others. Early in the reign a woman actually found her way unnoticed to the queen's room, and, entering unconcernedly, took a quiet survey of her Majesty and the Duchess of Ancaster, who was sitting with her. The two ladies were much taken aback by the visit, but the duchess having rung the bell, one of her pages came and showed the intruder downstairs. Nothing, however, seemed to make the officials exert due vigilance. In 1788 Princess Elizabeth was seated in her room, when she was alarmed by the sudden appearance of a man. She fled in terror by another door and gave the alarm to the attendants. One of the pages came and seized him, but he refused to give any account of himself or how he got admission. The porter said he could not have passed him. As usual, he was allowed to depart, but returned presently, insisting on seeing the princess, "that he might declare his passion and at her feet press for an equal return." He proved to be one Spang, a hairdresser, and of course mad. He had climbed the garden wall of the palace. Another of these odd suitors was Stone, who also declared his passion, presenting the queen with letters declaring "that they would make a very happy couple." No notice being taken, he appeared at St. James's, announcing that he considered his proposals as accepted, "for silence always gave consent." He, too, was found to be insane.

On another occasion in 1778, as the king was getting out of his chair near the back stairs of St. James's Palace, a woman rushed forward and attempted to lay hold of him. He with difficulty escaped from her, and then, in his usual quiet fashion, asked her who she was and what she wanted. She said flippantly that "she was Queen Beck." It came out, however, that she was a poor lunatic.

On another occasion a woman with a basket passed the porter at the gate, and contrived to leave the basket in one of the offices. It was found to contain a child two months old. The good-natured king had it brought to him, consigned it to a nurse, and directed it to be called by his own name. When the Perreaus, in 1776, for committing a forgery, were ordered for execution, the unhappy Mrs. Perreau with three of her children, all in deep black, contrived by some means to get admission to the palace, and to be posted where they could intercept her Majesty on her way to the chapel. The kind-hearted lady was deeply shocked when they cast themselves on their knees and held up. their petition with tears and lamentations, Mrs. Perreau exclaiming, "O mercy, mercy, my husband and their father!" Much affected, she received the petition and assured her it should reach the king. It was so done, but it was thought inadvisable that the convicts' lives should be spared.

The queen would often exercise a wholesome discretion in advising her ladies as to their acquaintances. Thus Miss Burney had formed an intimacy with Madame de Genlis, which her Majesty could not approve of. The French lady was ardently pressing Fanny to carry on a correspondence, and the queen sensibly advised her against it. "Had you begun it," she said, " perhaps you could not avoid carrying it on ; but as it is, it were safest to let it alone." She then told her how the lady had all but tormented her into granting her audience.

In the year 1782 the queen was sorely tried by the loss of her infant son. The young Prince Alfred had been sent down to Deal, as he was a very weakly child. The royal family were then on a round of visits to the nobility—to Lord Boston and the Duchess of Portland. The boy, however, died on August 20th, and was buried in Westminster Abbey, in the vault under Henry VII.'s Chapel. There lay the two coffins of the late king and queen together, the sides of the coffins being removed by direction of the king, so that the dust might mingle. On the 30th May in the following year, another of the family, Princess Octavius, died at Kew of the small-pox. These losses had been supplied by the recurring additions to the royal family, until it came to the year 1783, when her Majesty's fifteenth and last child was born—Princess Amelia. The royal lady had indeed done her duty by the State.

CHAPTER V.

COURT LIFE AND CHARACTERS.

ONE of the most remarkable pictures of the court life of the queen that we have is assuredly the minute and almost laboriously kept diary of Lady Mary Coke, recently published. This work fills four quartos of close print, and furnishes, without verbiage or affectation,[1] every incident of the day or night. The king, queen, princes and princesses, personages of every degree of rank pass before us ; all their sayings and doings are recorded, furnishing certainly a most extraordinary picture of manners and society. What strikes one particularly is the singularly low standard of morals, particularly among the ladies, and the positive effrontery that carried off the innumerable breaches of propriety and good conduct. The higher the rank, the more glaring and outrageous was the offence ; and though the queen was presumed to be a purist in regulating her court, she seemed to have been compelled to accept this state of things in a business-like fashion, and no doubt

[1] It has attracted little or no attention—possibly on account of its excessive amplitude, and because it has not been formally published.

thought that the evil was so deeply ingrained as to make reform hopeless. The author was a woman of remarkable force of character, of much power of will, though a most disagreeable specimen of her sex. Determined to yield to no one, and to force her own view on everybody, no matter what their position, she passed through the fashionable world, no doubt making her way by her cleverness, and the dread of attack that she inspired.

"She had the reputation," says Lady Louisa Stuart, "of cleverness while young, and could not be called a silly woman ; but she was so invincibly wrong-headed—her understanding lay smothered under so much pride, self-conceit, prejudice, obstinacy and violence of temper—that you never knew where to look for her. Her friendships were only lukewarm, and too zealous for the peace of the mortals upon whom they were bestowed—I might say inflicted."

She was a daughter of the house of Argyle, of the widowed duchess who had married the brilliant Charles Townshend and was created Baroness Greenwich. As candid as she was downright, she reveals her own failures and shortcomings with the utmost frankness. She was an inveterate gambler, and records with delight the parties—the only ones she seemed to enjoy—where she won sixteen, or lost thirty, or it may be sixty, guineas. It is astonishing the extent to which this practice prevailed among women—it seemed to be an accepted pastime. One of the king's sisters—Princess Amelia—was a deep player. In short, gambling, constant "going

off" with married dames, divorces, duels, were all
ordinary incidents of the time.

The story of this lady's marriage is dramatic, but painful. She had received a good offer from Mr. Coke, Lord
Leicester's son, a debauched young man, which of course
was no serious objection in those days, and as her family
was anxious for it, she appears to have set herself
resolutely against the match. Her young suitor had a
spirit to match her own, and showed himself thoroughly
careless whether she liked him or not.   Up to her
wedding day she affected all the airs of disgust and of
suffering compulsion " with a frozen mien, &c." After
the ceremony, when she was treating him the same way,
he coolly told her that she need be in no fear whatever
of tyrannous compulsion, that she might go her way and
do what she pleased, " and so made his bow and left her,
to her great mortification." The scenes of wedded life that
followed, as described by the vivacious Lady Louisa Stuart,
are almost amazing. She maintained her semi-dogged
front, made herself as odiously disagreeable to his family as
she could, and finally succeeded in setting not only his, but
her own family against her.   Her husband's father, who
had warmly taken up her cause against his son, she
forced to join his son against her, and they actually went
the length of imprisoning her in her room for months,
depriving her of money and liberty.   But nothing would
break her spirit.

One of the features in her very amusing diaries is the
view they give us of the various princes and princesses,

who were so freely ranging about society. What strikes us with astonishment—we who live in days where deference to "the royalties" is carried to an almost devout extent—is the familiar treatment of these great personages by the fashionable crowd. They seemed to be willing to push their way and seek amusement in all sorts of circles, just as other people would do.

Princess Amelia, the king's sister, was a good-tempered and amiable personage—altogether a very remarkable princess in many ways.[1] As Lady Louisa Stuart tells us, " she was a woman of quick parts and warm feelings, and saw further into Lady Mary's character, for she knew more of the world than princesses usually do ; partly from native sagacity, partly from keeping better company and having a mind above that jealous fear of the superior in understanding which so often leads them to prefer associating either with people of mean capacity, gratuitously dubbed *good creatures*, or else with those who can cunningly veil their sense and act the part of butts and buffoons for interested purposes."

With the indomitable Lady Mary Coke she cemented an intimate friendship which lasted for many years, and was based on a similarity of taste, a passion for gambling. The pair scarcely ever met at parties without the invariable game of " Lu," which seemed to be always

---

[1] So tolerant and good-natured was she that she allowed much to the oddities and familiar manners of her comrades, as when she complained of Lady Bateman, who was travelling with her in a chaise, and who "required to spit" so frequently that the glasses were every minute being put down.

attended by heavy loss. There were constant missives
commanding the lady's attendance at Gunnersbury ;
indeed, the royal dame seemed scarcely able to " get on "
without her friend, whose downright talk and criticisms
amused her.   But her forbearance was often severely
tried by the forwardness and even insolence not merely
of this friend, but of some of her ladies and intimates, who
seemed to treat her as if she were of their class.   Thus,
when a somewhat arrogant lady, Lady Harriet, her *dame
d'autour*, in 1768, openly grumbled because the princess
desired that her ladies should take their place according
to their rank, and not by seniority of appointment as was
claimed, she herself having come before two other ladies,
the tolerant princess appealed to her friends, asking
them if this were reasonable ?

One night there was a party at Lord Hereford's, when
on her arrival Mr. Walpole carried a lighted candle
before her upstairs.   When the card tables were being
made up for her usual " Loo," she was asked to name the
players for her table.   She always " did the correct
thing," and at first declined to make any choice—" so
careful is she not to give offence, and to be obliging to
all," said one of her friends ; but upon being desired a
second time, she said, " Then we will go according to
rank," and named the Duchess of Hamilton, Lady Hereford and others, but noticing a friend of hers, Mrs. Harris,
wife, I suppose, of Harris of Salisbury, she said good-
naturedly : " Oh, my poor dear Mrs. Harris, but I cannot
have you to-night."   The free-and-easy Duchess of

Hamilton then said pertly, "If you regret her so much, 'tis a pity you should not have her." The impertinence and ill breeding of the speech struck all the company. But the princess very quietly said to her, "Well, if you have a mind to go to the other table, I beg you will."

Even at her own house these insubordinate ladies treated her to their airs and humours. They were playing cards as usual, and a Mrs. Fitzroy had been dealing. One of her players asked her for five cards, when she said she would not give them. She was prevailed on by Mr. Walpole to give them, but said she would not pay the money, "and got into such a passion as to astonish all," and struck a deep silence. She then turned on Lady Mary Coke in the most violent manner, but that lady made her no reply. The royal hostess, thus insulted, could only whisper Lady Mary her praise for her self-restraint. It has always been noted that excessive gambling breaks down all barriers and breeds a sort of license and brutality of manners.

This agreeable princess was on the most free terms with her intimates, who answered her jests in a corresponding spirit. Once she suggested to Lord Bessborough that, as he was now left alone, owing to his daughter's marriage, he should get a wife, naming Lady Anne Howard as a suitable person. He said there was too much difference in their ages, but that if *she* would accept of him their ages would agree better; on which the princess laughed to such a degree that " she could scarcely stand." She then good-humouredly discussed the proposal.

Mr. Walpole described an odd scene at which he was present, and when the impetuous princess exhibited her curious humour. They were playing cards, she sitting opposite to him, when she asked abruptly, "How did you vote?" "Madam, I went away." "Upon my word," she said, scornfully, "that was *carving* well!" After an interval she asked him who a certain Sir E. Winnington just promoted was. "He is the late Mr. Winnington's heir." She said, "Who was a great Tory originally," and then asked what he was when he died. "Madam, I believe what all people in place are." On which she flew into a violent passion, coloured scarlet, and said, "None of your wit! I don't understand joking upon these subjects; if your father had heard you say it, he would have murdered you, and you would have deserved it." He was quite confounded and amazed at this public attack. It was impossible to explain across the table. She was so deaf. "I said to those beside me, 'What shall I do?'" However, on going away he whispered her that all he meant was that he supposed Tories were Whigs when they got office. She took it good-humouredly: "Oh, I am very much obliged to you, sir; indeed I was very angry."

On another occasion, before the queen's arrival, the princess was at a party at Bedford House, where there was for her limited Loo and unlimited for the Duchess of Grafton, with a table of quinze. Here was opportunity for the gamblers. French horns and clarionets played in the gardens. The princess had heard that the players

were served with cold meat set upon the Loo tables so
as to save time. She rather enjoyed the notion, and
desired to have the same served in that way. And so it
was done. And the entertainment went on, a mixture
of play and eating. "Think if King George the Second
could have risen and seen his daughter supping pell-mell
with men as it were in a booth." The tables were
removed ; the gay folk began to dance to fife and tabor ;
the ardent princess sat down once more, this time to
unlimited Loo, and played on till three in the morning.

This independent royal lady lived till she grew very
old, at her house in Cavendish Square—that which
stands at the corner of Harley Street—and which has
since been divided into smaller mansions. She used to
say that she was sure to die in October, as her father
had died in that month. As it turned out, she died on
the 31st, 1787, and was buried in Henry VII.'s Chapel.
She was the last surviving child of George II.

One of the queen's ladies who has been already introduced was the celebrated Duchess of Hamilton,
perhaps the most fortunate of all the beauties who have
figured at the English court. She was an extraordinary
personage, not so frivolous as her ill-fated sister, Lady
Coventry, but an *étourdie* in her own way. She had a
good deal of that careless recklessness so often found in
Irish girls—the "saying what came into her head"—
and eke doing it when it served the purpose of the
moment. This, however, served her instead of resolution and purpose, for she seemed to have no fear, no

shyness, and pushed forward to gain whatever she wanted. No lady ever succeeded in getting to herself so many of the honours of the peerage.

The duchess was known to have but little restraint, and Lady Charlotte Finch, the royal governess, complained that "she talked too much and improperly." She would start delicate matters before the king and queen, to extract their opinion, but the prudent king would never make her an answer. He knew "if he said a word it would be told all over the town." On occasions she would exhibit her ill humour in public, as at Lady Dundas's party, who "vowed and declared" that she should never be asked again.

When the Princess of Brunswick was in London in 1772, the queen, according to Mr. Walpole, became jealous of her and would never let her see the king alone. The Princess of Wales, her mother, had invited the princess to England; yet she was not allowed to lodge at Carlton House, or at St. James's Palace, which was empty, but at "a miserable little house in Pall Mall specially taken for her." Yet another stronger instance of the queen's "jealousy and haughtiness" was quoted. On the birthday, Lady Gower, who had been one of the princess's ladies, got the Duchess of Argyle to induce the Duchess of Hamilton to allow her a place beside the princess. The queen was displeased, and a day or two later in presence of the ladies said, " Duchess, I must reprimand you for letting Lady Gower take place of you, as lady to the Princess of Brunswick. I had a mind to speak to you on the spot, but would not, for fear of saying anything I should repent of, though I should have thought it. The Princess of Brunswick has nothing to do here, and I insist on your recovering the precedence you gave up. One day or other my son will be married, and then I shall have his wife's ladies pretending to take place in my palaces, which they shall not do."

All these oddities make her extraordinary and rude treatment of Boswell at Inverary intelligible. It has alway been incredible that a lady of such rank could behave so vulgarly to a guest who was under her roof. Of this noble dame it was said that the queen had even been jealous, and had used her so ill that she had thought of resigning. But her husband, as Walpole wrote, was a careful and wary man, who loved money better than her and was not jealous. "Whether as the duchess grew old and lost her beauty, and whether to disguise her own jealousy, the queen had made her a sort of favourite ; but the duchess had grown so insolent and behaved so familiarly with the king, even at chapel and behind the queen's chair, that the latter was determined to affront her ; and when she was to go to Warley Camp with the king, and it was the duchess's turn to wait, the queen said she would have Lady Egremont to go. The duchess was so angry that she went home and told the duke she would write and resign. The duke, the most cautious and interested of men, said she might resign, but he would dictate her letter. The wilful lady allowed him to do so, but added this post-script—'Though *I* write the letter, the duke dictated it.'" The sensible, tolerant queen bade her think over the matter, which she did, and kept her place. "The fortune of this woman," said Mr. Walpole, "was so extraordinary, that I have often thought it worth mentioning."

A little incident reveals in a highly characteristic fashion the queen's methods of domestic government and the strictness of her supervision. The Duchess of Hamilton was on one occasion late, and kept her royal mistress waiting. They were going to the play, and the excuse she made was that "she had *broke* her watch" and did not know the time. Not long after the queen presented her with a new one set with diamonds, adding, that "she would never be too late again." We are inclined to suspect that the excuse was a little fiction or was not the real one, but we must admire the royal character of the rebuke. The duchess, as we have said, had all the capricious carelessness of her countrywomen.

The extraordinary career of this lady has been often rehearsed. Fortune seems to have attended her every step. "I remember," says Lady Mary Coke, "once her saying that she never wished for anything that she had not had. 'Tis some comfort for those who have not been so favoured with success, to observe that it is not always the most deserving that are the most prosperous in this world." As is well known, she was "a double duchess"—that is of Hamilton and Argyle,

besides being made a baroness in her own right. She
also became mother of two Dukes of Hamilton and of
two Dukes of Argyle.

Between the impulsive Duchess—first the wife of
the Marquis of Lorne—and the eccentric Lady Mary
Coke there was a continuous quarrel going on. Lady
Mary always speaks of her with rage and hostility, and
bore her a bitter grudge for some injury done—likely
enough an interference with her plans of capturing
the Duke of York. After one of the queen's confine-
ments, Lady Mary, according to the custom of the time,
went to the palace to inquire after her Majesty, whose
friends it appears were allowed to walk in and out, make
their way into the drawing-rooms—and even into her
Majesty's bedroom. "Who should be in waiting but
the Duchess of Hamilton? But I behaved as you would
have wished me, put all her impertinence out of my
mind, went up and without any particular look or manner
desired to know how her Majesty did. She did not
do the same ; her look and manner were so extraordinary
that all the ladies in the room were near laughing. I
believe she answered me, but I can't tell you what she
said." We find Lady Mary Coke incessantly attributing
to her all kinds of evil turns. "She has been so much
my enemy," she says. However, it is pleasant to tell
that in 1790, when the famous duchess was on her
death-bed, the old enemies were reconciled. Lady Mary
was assiduous in her attendance on the once beauty—and
indeed was the only person admitted. In her diary she

records her deep grief. This is creditable to both. They were in fact two high-spirited and much-spirited dames.

Almost everything that we hear of this erratic duchess is quite in character. When the Wilkes excitement was strong and a shouting mob had gathered round St. James's Palace, where the king was, the duchess sent off to the queen's house, to inquire " how her Majesty did after her fright." The queen, who knew nothing of this incident— the king not having yet returned—was greatly alarmed until the matter was explained to her. These were the acts of an *étourdie*—a not uncommon type, whose ideas outstrip words and reflection. In 1767 it was known that she had asked for a peerage for herself—it was said indeed, " there was nothing she would not ask for "—and she actually obtained it.

During one of the services at the chapel, Lady Mary declared that she could not help recalling a capital dinner she had just had, and which consisted of " a noodle soup," i.e. " a soup of veal with lumps of bread boiled in it, a hash of mutton, and a tongue, with greens, and spinach and eggs,"—not very refined fare for a court dame. On another occasion she recorded : " I don't remember ever to have seen her Majesty *talk so much* during a service." Many odd things seem to have occurred during these services—such as the adventure of Squire Kynaston, described by the scurrilous Walcot,—

> " When, after prayers, so good and rare a sermon,
> He found his front attacked by fierce Miss Vernon,
> Who, in God's house, without one grain of grace,
> Spit like a vixen in his worship's face."

Miss Vernon was one of the queen's maids of honour.

Lady Mary was ambitious and flew at high game. It is clear that she made a deep impression on the king's brother, the Duke of York, who was always " hovering " about her and constantly coming to see her. This attachment was laughed at by the court, and by her many enemies. But it is certain from the diaries, where she minutely chronicles his visits and conversations, that there was good foundation for her hopes. His unfortunate and premature death abroad, she took deeply to heart, and exhibited her grief rather publicly. She at least felt the disappointment acutely. The royal family were particularly sarcastic on these exhibitions, and gave out that it was a mere theatrical display to make herself of importance.

She had actually wept over his coffin, widow-like. It was said that at a meeting between her and the Princess Emily, when she was giving way to this affectation of grief, that downright personage said to her coolly, " My good Lady Mary, if you did but know what a joke he used to make of you to us, you would soon have done crying for him ! " The other was not likely to forgive this thrust.

Under all difficulties, the queen's good humour never deserted her; she was always ready to carry off the situation with a smile or a pleasant speech. Thus, at a Drawing Room in 1769 she was talking to Lady Mary, and was " very civil " to her, when, in retiring,

Lady Mary's petticoat got entangled in the queen's. Extrication became difficult and took long, when the lady tore her own. The queen smiled at this rather awkward *contretemps*, and said, "Lady Mary seems to have no mind to part with me!"

In Holy Week of 1769, Lady Mary refused to go to her patroness the princess, as she could not bring herself to play cards on that day. The princess was highly displeased, and told her that she had never intended playing cards, and later on in the evening the offended Lady Mary heard her whisper to a lady, "Pharisee!" "from which I conclude H.R.H. meant to insinuate that I pretended to be better than others."

Lady Louisa Stuart in her own lively way describes how the inevitable breach between the princess and her friend came about, which was perhaps about the year 1781.

"It is an ugly lineament in human nature, but certainly friendships—or what the world calls so—are subject to the wear and tear of time. Old companions do insensibly grow tired of hearing each other's faults and infirmities and suppressing their own; as if on both sides ill humour, waxing larger, wanted more elbow-room. The princess and Lady Mary were almost arrived at this dangerous point. Nobody could be easier to live with than the former, but she would have the respect due to her observed, and as dispute and contradiction now and then went the length of downright impertinence, her royal highness's patience began to be on

the ebbing side. Lady Mary set down the cards one
evening in a mood of superlative perverseness, sought
occasion to squabble, found fault with the princess's play,
laughed her assertions to scorn, and finally got a very
sharp reply for her pains. In lieu of recollecting herself,
she took fire and retorted more sharply still. The princess declined further altercation with an air that said,
'I remember who I am,' and the company glared at each
other in silence. When the party broke up, Lady Mary
departed unspoken to, and all concluded that she would
be admitted to that house no more. But Princess
Emily gave her fairer play than they expected. She
desired to see her alone, and calmly entered upon a
good-humoured expostulation. 'We are such old
friends,' said she, 'that it is really too foolish to fall out
and part about a trifle, but you must be conscious you
were very provoking the other night. As I lost my
temper too, I am the readier to forgive; only say you are
sorry, and I will never think of it again.' Lady Mary
drew herself up to her utmost height, and answered,
'Madam, I respect your royal highness as I ought, but
I cannot give up my integrity and honour. I cannot
retract opinions I have once delivered, while I continue
persuaded they are just. Your royal highness yourself
would despise me did I act so meanly. I am no syco-
phant, no flatterer—adulation will never flow from me.'
'Pooh, pshaw, nonsense!' cried the princess. 'Where
is the use of all these heroics about nothing? Who
wants you to retract or flatter, and I know not what?

Can't you say, as I say myself, that you are concerned for this very silly business, and so let us be friends?'
'No, madam, my honour—my honour, which is dearer to me than life—' And then followed another tirade. After one or two more endeavours to bring her down from her stilts, the other rose to *her* full height likewise, and assuming all the dignity of the king's daughter, 'Well, madam,' she said, 'your ladyship knows your own pleasure best—I wish you health and happiness for the future, and at present a good morning. Here,' to the page-in-waiting, 'order Lady Mary Coke's carriage,'—then gravely bowing in token of dismissal, turned away. From that moment they never met again. The loss was altogether Lady Mary's, and also hers the reproach. This was betrayed by a constant fidgety anxiety to know what was going on at Princess Emily's parties."

The remarkable thing about this strange scene was the perfect equality assumed by the combatants, in the face of the high rank of one of the parties. The wrangle had taken place in the presence of a mixed company, and seems to have been accepted as an ordinary incident. Naturally, when princesses came down from their high pedestal this was to be expected. There is, however, no such leveller as gaming; and the passion of greed, loss, disappointment banishes all restraint, and all respect.

This extraordinary dame continued to the last to exhibit her untamable disposition. It would almost seem that she had abdicated all control, or rather had accepted and took pride in the hateful tyranny of her own will. Abroad, both at the French and Austrian courts, she was made a great deal of, and was received into the intimate society of the empress-queen, and the French king and queen. But soon the old ill-conditioned nature asserted itself. At Vienna she took a dislike or hatred to an important lady, whom she strove to over-throw. The empress took the side of the lady, and gave the stranger a sharp set down. The courtiers followed suit, and fell away from her. Hence she raged with fury against the great lady, who, she fancied, was engaged in plots to ruin her. It was the same wherever she went. A friendship of a long series of years was a sufficient challenge to her to pick a quarrel and change it into bitter animosity. In the confusion and bickerings that grew out of the irregular marriages of the Dukes of Cumberland and Gloucester, she took a prominent part.[1]

The escapades of the maids of honour and other ladies about the court must have also brought serious trouble and anxiety to the excellent queen. These persons seemed of the most unsteady, volatile character; but the truth was, authority was weak, and the selection was not always made with judgment. There were constant changes taking place owing to elopements, forbidden marriages and other reasons. The Duchess of Hamilton, as we have seen, was an indiscreet choice. In 1768 we hear of one of the maids of honour—Miss Meadows, sister to Lord Manvers—running off to make a stolen marriage with Captain Campbell, a penniless officer, and

[1] She died in 1811.

without giving notice to the queen or to her father. The worthy king set to work to patch up this affair— sent for the father to ask him to be reconciled to his daughter, while notice was given to the young lady that she was not to come to court until she had " made it up" with her family. Such pressure was not to be resisted, and his Majesty succeeded in his laudable aim. Then the queen generously gave her late maid of honour a present of £1000, which has since grown into an established custom or right. Miss Varnon, or Vernon, succeeded Miss Meadows.[1]

The queen had always been fond of cards for the pleasure of playing ; but for some years, as we have seen, it would not be tolerated at the palace. At last, in 1768, she succeeded in introducing them, and had, in a quiet domestic way, her game with the king, Lady C. Finch, the Duchess of Ancaster and others of the *entourage*. Nothing she enjoyed more.

[1] Lady M. Coke's Diaries.

CHAPTER VI.

THE ROYAL HOUSEHOLD AND COURT.

THE royal children were brought up in a very simple way at Kew under the direction of their governess. The young Prince of Wales when not more than four or five years old was a most precocious child. One day " Lady Mary," coming to pay a visit to Lady C. Finch, found him at dinner. He asked her to sit by the table, and confided to her that " he did not like his dinner, as it was not his meat day." He then insisted on her playing with him until it grew very late, when she told him she was going to his aunt, Princess Amelia, at Gunnersbury, when he put the odd question, " Pray are you well-dressed enough to visit her ? " He then ordered her servants, and announced that he would go downstairs with her to the door.

The Duke of Montague, who succeeded Lord Holdernesse as governor of the royal children, left among his papers the following routine of diet for the year 1776. It was very strictly regulated. " For breakfast there was simple milk or a basin two-thirds milk and one of tea, moderately sweetened, and dry toast of the Statute bread.

QUEEN CHARLOTTE

(*From the picture by West*)

Breakfast was at half-past nine, dinner from three to five, supper at half-past eight. On Mondays they had no supper, and every alternate Monday was bathing night. At dinner, soup if they chose it, when not very strong or heavy—any plain meat without fat of one sort, clear gravy and greens, of which they eat what they please. Fish when they please, but without butter, using the shrimps strained from the sauce or oil and vinegar. At the second course they eat the fruit of the tart without crust. Peas or what other simple thing they chose, but of one only. At the dessert on Sundays and Thursdays they eat ice of what sort they chose. Coffee allowed only on these two days, and one glass of any sort of wine they chose after dinner. For dress they had six suits of full dress clothes a year, various common suits, new boots spring and fall ; new shoes each fortnight, new hats as wanted, but always four silver-looped, gold-looped, and two plain besides the Arm Hat."

It will be noted that certain days were meat days. When the princes were older and reached the ages of thirteen and fourteen the same simple diet was continued.

At Kew, the eldest young princes went regularly every day at five o'clock to pay a visit to their parents, at the Lodge. They drove in a little chaise that just held them, and were suffered to go without their governess. At half-past six Lady Charlotte Finch was expected to visit the royal pair and remain till nine, but not later; for the queen did not like the king to be out after that hour, and he submitted with good-natured complaisance, though he would have liked to continue his walks later.

An illustration of the frivolous pretences on which a quarrel was engendered may be quoted from Lady M. Coke's Diary. The scene was a birthday ball at the queen's house. Lords Delawarr and Huntingdon were talking, when Mr. Errington of Northumberland passed by. Lord Delawarr asked who he was, when his companion told him he was a Catholic gentleman whose family had been rebels, "like yours and mine, my Lord," he added. Lord Delawarr answered warmly that he knew of none such in his family, on which the other begged his pardon for saying so, and then added significantly, "if that did not do,—why he was ready to give him any other kind of satisfaction that he desired."—"If you please, my lord, I'll meet you after the levée to-morrow," the other answered promptly. "Why put it off so long? I desire you will meet me before the levée." How incredible seems this—and who could imagine two noble-men of this country picking a quarrel on such futile pretext? It shows what a frivolity and "lack of bottom," as Johnson would call it, did then obtain. It chanced that the inconsequent Duchess of Hamilton overheard some of the dialogue, and went to tell the queen. The queen told the king, who sensibly interposed, threatening the two bellicose lords with arrest ; and so they were compelled to "make up" the matter.

The queen was always generous in recognizing service, and often her presents to a retainer were of a truly regal kind. Witness her gift to one of her ladies, the Duchess of Ancaster—her own picture set in a medallion in a frame of diamonds, with a crown on the top in precious stones. This was worn at the side of the waist at the end of a broad sash, like an order. The queen herself wore the king's portrait in the same fashion.[1]

It was extraordinary what a number of levées there were then at St. James's Palace during the winter. Two were held every week, on Wednesday and Friday, and often a third. The queen usually had her drawing-room every Thursday, and at which the king was always present, so that he thus devoted some four mornings out of seven during the greater portion of the year to this ceremonial. The object was, I fancy, to find opportunities for talk with the leading personages, for much was

[1] The poor queen little dreamed that some twenty years after her death she should be wantonly selected by a Frenchman as the subject of a good " fat " scandal. One scribbler who wrote the stirring drama of the " Tower of Nesle " in conjunction with A. Dumas, took up the subject of the Chevalier d'Eon, and casting about him for something to add " spice " to his adventures, introduced the young Queen Charlotte of England as his admirer. In 1836 two volumes were issued by this writer of an authentic kind. Papers were obtained from the family and from the public archives, and a rather interesting work we are assured was the result. But as the late Mr. Thom pointed out, a notice that appeared in the second edition is one of the most astounding confessions that we know. The author tells his readers very candidly that such a complicated and exciting life as that of the Chevalier *must* have had many romantic and secret passages which have not come to light, which he, therefore, as a young man of imagination, felt bound to supply from his own fancy. " I believed, all in good faith, that I had come on the track of these amours in the letters of audiences accorded by the young Queen of England to the Chevalier, after the peace of 1763," and this theme he developed in a series of thoroughly French scenes.

done at this period by "talk," and the king was a tremendous talker. He never seemed to tire. When she seemed extenuated by fatigue, his Majesty would start off into an endless chat with an ambassador or some courtier—often thus detaining her more than half an hour longer. As was to be expected, these receptions were but thinly attended. Sometimes the king found " no house," or that only a few had arrived ; and he would then send out his groom of the chambers to report. The levées were held in a small bedroom—usually the one in which James II.'s son was born. Next to it was " the king's closet," where the more confidential communications took place. The foreign ministers stood in a row from the bed to the door, and the king advanced, talking to each. A crowd gathered at the door, waiting for notice. As the king talked with one, he was adroitly scanning the next in order and preparing himself for his next dialogue. The queen displayed a true dignity and condescension at these ceremonies.

This year the Countess Dowager of Effingham, one of the ladies of her Majesty's bedchamber, died of a fright she received by her clothes taking fire at her apartments in Hampton Court.

" Their Majesties were now accustomed to rise at six o'clock in the morning, and enjoy the two succeeding hours, which they called their own : at eight the Prince of Wales, the Bishop of Osnaburg, the Princess Royal, and Princes William and Henry were brought from their separate houses to Kew House, to breakfast with their illustrious relations. At nine their younger children attended to lisp or smile their good morrows; and while the five eldest were close applying to their tasks, the little ones and their nurses passed the whole morning in Richmond Gardens. When the weather was unfavourable in the morning, the queen employed herself with needlework.

" The king and queen frequently amused themselves by sitting in the room while the children dined; and, once a week, attended by the whole offspring in pairs, made the little tour of Richmond Gardens. In the afternoon the queen worked, and the king read to her: all the children again paid their duty at Kew House before they retired to bed, and the same order was preserved through each returning day. Topography was one of the king's favourite studies; he copied every capital chart, took the models of all the celebrated fortifications, knew the soundings in the chief harbours in Europe, and strong and weak sides of the most fortified towns. He could name every ship in his navy, and kept lists of his commanders; and all these were private acquisitions of his own choosing.

" The Prince of Wales and the Bishop of Osnaburg made a rapid progress in learning: eight hours' close application to the languages and the liberal sciences, were the tasks daily allotted to their royal highnesses.

" Exercise, air, and little diet were the grand fundamentals in the king's idea of health and sprightliness: his Majesty fed chiefly on vegetables, and drank little wine.

The queen was what many private gentlewomen styled whimsically abstemious; for at a table covered with dainties, she culled the plainest and the simplest dish, and seldom ate of more than two things at a meal.[1]   Her wardrobe was changed every three months, and her greatest care was that English manufactures should be provided for her wear.   The Duchess of Kingston, when the Hon. Miss Chudleigh, and one of the maids of honour, had often assisted her Majesty's wardrobe, and who was allowed to be the richest queen of Europe in that respect.   The tradesmen's bills were regularly paid once a quarter for what came under the children's department.

" The king and queen, during their daily walks or rides, were assiduous in discovering objects of compassion, and equally ready in giving their assistance whenever distress wanted relief, or industry encouragement.   The queen was not only the *mother* of orphans, having clothed, educated, and provided for fifty daughters of officers in the army, and fifty daughters of officers in the navy, from the age of six to eighteen; but also the friend of destitute widows, to a certain number of whom she allowed annual pensions according to their ranks.   The king never talked of state affairs to the queen; indeed Lord Chesterfield believed he never spoke a word of politics to her."

Few sovereigns have had a more correct and ardent

[1] At the 1784 Egham races, which their Majesties visited, the royal pair were seen to take their lunch in homely fashion before the crowd—of " cold beef, ham and veal."   They appeared to heartily enjoy this plain repast.

taste for music than their Majesties; the works of Handel being in the highest favour, and enjoyed with almost enthusiasm. The private band of the palace was not a mere ornamental portion of the establishment, but played several nights in the week for the private enjoyment of the royal pair. They had their favourite pieces and were good critics.

This musical taste was further shown by the royal encouragement of an important musical development which took place in the year 1784, when the system of "Festivals," which has done so much for music in England, was inaugurated on a grand scale. This might be considered a particular homage to Handel, in whose honour the whole project was conceived and happily worked out. A few "persons of distinction" had conceived the idea of a festival, and consulted with the directors of the "Concerts of Ancient Music," who entertained it ; but the king coming to hear of it, took up the project warmly.

The temporary building in the abbey was comprised within the west aisle, and large enough to receive four thousand persons. At the upper end, a throne was erected in the Gothic style, with a centre box for the royal family; another box on one side for the bishops and dignitaries of the Church, and a third for the foreign ambassadors. The orchestra was built at the opposite extremity, ascending regularly, from the height of about seven feet above the floor, to forty feet from the ground; extending also from the centre to the top of the side

aisles, and so admirably constructed, that Bates, who
presided at the new and magnificent organ, could see
and be distinctly seen by the whole of the numerous
band.   The intermediate space was filled with level
benches appropriated to the subscribers, and the side
aisles were formed into long galleries ranging with the
orchestra, and ascending, so as to contain twelve rows
on each side.

On Wednesday, the 26th of May, was the festival,
and before ten in the morning the company assembled
in prodigious numbers, so that in about an hour the
venerable pile was nearly filled, chiefly with ladies.
Their Majesties arrived about a quarter past twelve
o'clock ; and when the king came into his box, " he stood
for some moments seemingly lost in astonishment at the
sublimity of the spectacle ; nor did the brilliancy of
the appearance less affect the feelings of the queen, who
viewed it with rapture, and repeatedly expressed her
admiration to those around her.

" The festival then began with the Coronation Anthem,
in the execution of which were fully displayed the
amazing powers of the band, consisting of more than
five hundred performers.   Mr. Bates, who was the
conductor of the whole, appeared throughout *so agitated
and inflamed by the subject, that his instrument, though
immense in its tones, could hardly give utterance to his ideas.*

" On the following evening, the festival was renewed at
the Pantheon, which presented a most beautiful appearance; the dome being illuminated with seven thousand

lamps, in compartments, and terminating at the top of the cupola in a beautiful figure.

" In this night's performance, Madame Mara displayed all the wonders of her voice, which reached even the compass of an instrument. The selection of pieces did infinite credit to the directors, and the execution was such as to leave no room for criticism. Mr. Bates played the organ with the same touch as he did at the abbey, and the harmony in all the parts was complete.

" The next day was employed in the rehearsal of the Messiah, which masterpiece of Handel was performed at the abbey on the 29th. Their Majesties were attended by five princesses ; and it was evident throughout the whole of the performance how much they enjoyed the delicious banquet.

" On the 3rd of June, the performance, by the command of the king, consisted of a selection made under the direction of his Majesty ; and on the 5th of the same month the commemoration concluded with the Messiah, by order of the queen, when, though the crowd was less than on the preceding occasion, the exhibition was more splendid. There was an ingenious device in the manner of executing the music to 'Lift up your heads, O ye gates,' by causing the whole chorus from each side of the orchestra, in conjunction with all the instruments, to burst forth at once, 'He is the King of Glory,' which had such an admirable effect, as to bring tears into the eyes of several of the performers themselves. Nor was this effect confined to the orchestra : the whole auditory

felt a sympathetic emotion ; and his Majesty was
pleased to make the signal himself for the repetition of
this, and the final chorus in the last part. Thus ended
this grand festival, the like of which had never been exhibited in any country ; nor is it probable that anything
on such a scale will ever again recur.

" The royal donation to the fund on this occasion was
five hundred guineas, and the receipts exceeded twelve
thousand pounds, out of which six thousand were given
to the society for decayed musicians, and one thousand
to the hospital."

It is interesting to find that the amiable and sprightly
Dr. Burney was engaged to write a history of these
striking performances, to which his Majesty contributed
some passages that show a sound criticism. Dr. Burney
was one of the most engaging figures of the period, and
it is an odd pleasure to think that I was remotely connected with his family, though at some cost, having for
many years to pay a rent-charge to the descendants of
his daughter, Mrs. Philips.

The king and queen had also a genuine and cultured
taste for the stage, in its best and most refined forms,
notably that of comedy. They were true patrons of
the drama, and were indifferent to the vulgar conditions
of show and state, looking only to the intellectual
enjoyment. In some tiny, shabby country theatre they
enjoyed themselves as heartily as at Covent Garden.
Once talking over the play with Miss Burney, the queen
asked her " if she had seen one just come out, called

'He's much to Blame;' and began to relate its plot and characters, the representation and its effect; and, warming herself by her own account and my attention, she presently entered into a very minute history of each act, and a criticism upon some incidents, with a spirit and judiciousness that were charming. She is delightful in discourse when animated by her subject, and speaking to auditors with whom, neither from circumstance nor suspicion, she has restraint. But when, as occasionally she deigned to ask my opinion of the several actors she brought in review, I answered I had never seen them—neither Mrs. Pope, Miss Betterton, Mr. Murray, &c.—*she really looked almost concerned.* 'I,' she graciously said, 'prefer plays to all other amusements.'"

The royal pair were even interested in the players, and had their favourite " characters," which they would see again and again ; the king had his special comic performers, notably Quick, whom he would greet cordially and familiarly when he met him in public. Elliston was another favourite, while Mrs. Siddons was treated with a respectful homage suited to the stage and dignity of that great *tragedienne.*

There were then in country towns numerous small theatres which belonged to particular "circuits," and that at Richmond, and above all at Weymouth, enjoyed a large share of royal patronage. They were little " bandboxes " of houses, holding comparatively few, and but rudely fitted up ; but the royal party only cared to enjoy the *acting*. Nothing could be more simple and homely than these dramatic evenings.[1]

In nothing did they more delight than having a recital of a play at the palace, where John Kemble and his gifted sister would give, say, " The Jealous Wife," with the finest expression and elocution, though certainly without the airy comedy touch the piece required. It might be said that no new piece of reputation was brought out at the great theatres without being seen by their Majesties. They would attend in full force, and the spectacle of the long range of young princesses, who attended their parents, was as interesting to the audience as the figures on the stage.

In December, 1773, Stone, the queen's treasurer, died. He had been a Jacobite, and had a curious history. There were many candidates and much intriguing for the place. General Graeme reckoned on it, declaring that he had an actual promise. Sir George Macartney and George Selwyn, whose father had been Queen Caroline's treasurer, were particularly anxious to obtain it, but the latter was warned by his friends that one of his satirical nature was not likely " to be admitted into the mysterious and discreet penetralia of the queen's house." He persisted, however, and reminded Lord North of the promise that had been given. Lord North declared he had mentioned the matter to the king, who

---

[1] Once, at Weymouth, on a sultry afternoon, the king strayed into the theatre, sat down in his royal box and fell asleep ; the vivacious Elliston had to play his fiddle to rouse him.

said that he recollected nothing of the matter, and, adds Mr. Walpole, "the Duke of Grafton's veracity was more doubtful than even his Majesty's." Graeme was offended at not being named to the vacant place, and resigned his offices of secretary and comptroller to the queen. The secretaryship was at once conferred on Mr. Harris "of Malmsbury," a distinguished writer and philosopher, who held it till his death. Colonel Graeme, who no doubt fancied that her Majesty ought to have been under obligations to him for the part he had taken in selecting her for the throne, was consoled with the lucrative office of master of St. Catherine's Hospital.

In 1780 the king was sorely distressed by the revolt, as it might be termed, of two of his brothers, who in defiance of his authority had contracted secret marriages with subjects. The Duke of Gloucester had espoused Lady Waldegrave; and the Duke of Cumberland, Mrs. Horton. These marriages were not declared for some time. The king and queen were highly displeased, and forbade them to come into their presence.

Lady Louisa Stuart, that keen observer to whom we owe so many pleasant traits of this period, gives this sketch of the two ambitious dames :—" Lady Waldegrave was a most lovely woman, not of much sense, but blameless in character and conduct. She had the manners of high society, in which she had always moved; she was the widow of a distinguished man of quality, but there was no disguising it—the illegitimate daughter of Sir Edward Walpole. The widow Horton had no stain of birth, but in every other respect was far less fit for a princess. Lady Margaret Fordice said very aptly that after hearing the Duchess of Cumberland talk for half an hour, one ought to go home and *wash one's ears.*"

She was described by the same lady as vulgar, noisy, indelicate, and intrepid : " utter strangers to good company, they were never to be seen in any woman of fashion's house, though often leaders of riotous parties at Vauxhall. She belonged to that disgusting class of women who have never blushed in their lives, who because they have done nothing take the liberty of saying everything.

" Nothing could ever place her on a level with persons born in the purple, therefore she bore them an inveterate hatred. Her sister Betsy, or Lady Elizabeth Luttrell, who had a great deal of real though coarse wit, governed the family with a high hand, marshalled the gaming table, gathered round her the men, and led the way in ridiculing the king and queen. And a mighty scope for satire was afforded by the queen's wide mouth and occasionally imperfect English, as well as by the king's trick of saying, ' What ? What ? ' his ill-made coats, and general antipathy to fashion. But the marks generally aimed at were his virtues, his freedom from vice, above all, his religious *prejudices.* Nothing of this scoffing kind passed at Gloucester House."

Lady Mary Coke, she goes on, " ran some risk of losing her wits by these alliances. She foamed at the mouth, as she declaimed against them." She was " Duchess

Dowager of York by her own creation;" that is, she had, as we have seen, set her cap at the late duke, but unsuccessfully. Yet here were two attempts of the kind that had been successful. This inflamed her.

It was an extraordinary state of things to find no less than two of the king's brothers under the ban of the court, and setting up courts of their own, to which they strove to attract all comers, making a regular faction against the king. Highly offended, his Majesty, as Lady L. Stuart tells us, forbade them his sight, and notified that no one who frequented their courts should be received at St. James's. " This distressed the Duke of Gloucester, who was a favourite of the king's. And they were careful in their proceedings to observe a certain measure of respect and reserve. The duchess maintained a degree of state that gave some stiffness to her parties, which were commonly rather select. But in their case the ostracism did not last very long, for the king was much too good-natured to enforce his edict, especially against the Duke of Gloucester, whom he loved. His displeasure overawed people for the first month; in the second they stole a visit to Gloucester and Cumberland House, went to court early in the third, and being spoken to, troubled their heads no more about the matter." To prevent such scandals in the future the well-known Royal Marriage Act was passed.

CHAPTER VII.

THERE are many accounts of the queen in her social life, when she relaxed—mostly by journeymen hands with but little power of catching the diverse *measures* of characters. There is one artist, however, who has used her pen in limning her Majesty with the most signal effect, and her account of her first introduction at Windsor is so stored with delicate touches and the lighter graces of character, that it would be difficult to find anything that could furnish a better idea of this admirable and amiable lady. Though the queen had formed an opinion that Miss Burney's style was somewhat too delicate for the rough atmosphere of the stage, it may be said that her sketch of the first interview with their Majesties would do credit to any of the official professors in that age of good comedy writing. The picture is presented by the aid of a series of minute touchings : we have the most delicate shadings and gradations of tone. We can almost hear the queen's voice, and see what she would express by her gestures and glances.

I feel, of course, some hesitation in presenting once more these familiar and oft-quoted records, which every lover of sprightly writing and dramatic character knows by heart. But nowhere is Queen Charlotte presented so faithfully or with so many minute touches. Among the rather profuse surroundings and the numerous personal details with which the lively Fanny entertains us, the queen's figure is rather overpowered; but separated from them, it stands out with more effect, as it seems to me. I shall therefore make no further apology for drawing upon these memoirs.

Miss Burney, as the world knows, was a favourite of that venerable lady, Mrs. Delany, and Mrs. Delany was *persona gratissima* at court. Owing to her accounts of her charge, and also to their great interest in new books and writers of the time, the royal pair showed much curiosity to see the young authoress.

The good feeling and affection of the queen for her friend was exhibited in one very touching way. Mrs. Delany cherished a favourite bird that had belonged to her deceased duchess—a weaver bird it was called—but which was found one morning by Miss Burney lying dead in its cage. Miss Planta chanced to come in at this moment, and on her return reported her loss to the queen. Within a quarter of an hour she returned with another "weaver bird," which the queen happened to possess, and which she suggested might be substituted for the dead bird. She thought the aged lady might not notice any change. But it was found that the birds were so different that the change would be detected at once, and it was thought better to inform her of her loss ; but it was anticipated that the queen's kindly attempt would console her : and so it proved. Among other presents the queen gave her " an ingenious and elegant loom for making fringe," and a case of specially made instruments to help her in her " curious works "—the making of artificial flowers.

Miss Burney was on a visit to Mrs. Delany in November, 1785, and the king and queen were perpetually dropping in to have a long chat, all in the most friendly and delightfully familiar way. They were still eager to see her favourite, but there were many disappointments. The volatile Fanny affected to be full of terror at the impending awful *rencontre*.

At last one evening the king " dropped in." She tried to escape, but he asked in a loud whisper, " Was that Miss Burney ? " and then began to talk or chatter in his usual style. He asked her many curious questions about her writing, and she soon was at her ease. Later on the queen suddenly appeared. Miss Planta stepped out backwards, and reappeared with a candle, ushering her in. "Oh, your Majesty is here ! " she cried ; then welcomed her friend with both hands : " My dear Mrs. Delany, how are you ? " but her quick eye detected Fanny, and measured her, guessing who she was. The latter was " ready to sink." The good king saw her distress, and interposed with a sort of introduction : " I have been telling Miss Burney," &c., he said. The queen here dropped a curtsey with a very smiling and encouraging countenance. His Majesty went on repeating everything the young lady had said. Baretti, he repeated, had said that a man *must* be the writer of her novel, because no woman could ever have kept the secret.

The queen laughed, and said " that was quite too bad, and an affront to us." Then turning to the shy authoress, " Don't you think so ? " " addressing me with great gentleness of voice." It will be seen their Majesties were great admirers of the novels. And the queen had " Cecilia " read aloud to her by M. de Luc, who, it was added humorously, " could hardly speak four words of English." The queen, in her gay, lively fashion, " ran on " from topic to topic, and leaves the impression that she must have been a very agreeable talker. She used to declare that what she dreaded were people who merely said " yes " and " no," in answer to her questions or suggestions. She wished others to keep up the ball, otherwise she had not only to talk herself, but to maintain the whole conversation. She loved to hear free opinions freely expressed. An excellent specimen of her pleasant methods was exhibited on this meeting with Miss Burney. Describing the fog that filled the palace at a late Drawing Room, she drew some amusing pictures of her companions. " I assure you, ma'am," cried she to Mrs. Delany, " it was so dark, there was no seeing anything, and no knowing anybody. And Lady Harcourt could be of no help to tell me who the people were ; for when it is light she can't see, and when dark I cannot see myself. So it was in vain for me to go on in that manner, without knowing which I had spoken to and which was waiting for me ; so I said to Lady Harcourt, ' We had better stop, and stand quite still, for I don't know anybody no more than you do. But if we stand still, they will all come up in the end, and we must ask them who they are, and if I have spoken to them yet or not : for it is very odd to do it. But what else can we manage ? ' "

" Her accent," adds Miss Burney, " is a little foreign, and very prettily so ; and her emphasis has that sort of changeability which gives an interest to everything she utters. But her language is rather peculiar than foreign.

" She then gave an account of some circumstances which attended the darkness, *in a manner not only extremely lively, but mixed at times with an archness and humour that made it very entertaining.* She chiefly addressed herself to Mrs. Delany ; and to me certainly she would not separately have been so communicative : but she contrived with great delicacy to include me in the little party, by frequently looking at me, and always with an expression that invited my participation in the conversation."

In this clever little description there is a nice analysis of the queen's methods. We all must have met winning, gentle natures like this. When will not speech or action, by mere power of winning expression and an air of goodwill, take in, as it were, into their sympathy all about them ?

" Well," she continued, "there was standing by me
a man that I could not see in the face, but I saw the twist-
ing of his bow, and I said to Lady Harcourt, ' I am sure
that must be the Duke of Dorset.' ' Dear,' she says, ' how
can you tell that ? ' ' Only ask,' said I ; and so it proved to
be." In all which gossip there is a pleasant spontaneous
fluency. Her Majesty had evidently a turn for seeing
things and for putting things in a humorous light. Here,
too, was shrewd observation. The duke had had
a stroke, and had been obliged to hold his hand to
his mouth to hide it—"which he refuses to acknowledge was paralytic. The queen looked as if some
comic notion had struck her, and, after smiling a little
while to herself, said with a sort of innocent archness very pleasing, ' To be sure it is wrong to laugh
at such things—I know that ; but yet I could not
help thinking when his mouth was in that way, that
it was very lucky people's happiness did not depend
upon his smiles. ' "

She went on with her pleasant commentaries : " A lady
came up to me, but I could not see, so I was forced to
ask who she was ; and immediately she burst into a
laugh. ' Oh,' says I, ' that can be only Mrs. de Rolles ; '
and so it proved."

Miss Burney was now drawing off into her shy
retirement, when the queen delicately and in a half-
whisper said, "But shall we have no more—nothing
more ? " The heroine, always full of herself, and the
" dread importance " of the matter of her being known

to write, "could not but understand her, and only shook my head," a rather familiar fashion of enlightening the queen on the point.   Not unnaturally the queen thought she had said too much, and that the young lady was *froisséed.* "To be sure," she said, " it is, I own, a very home question for one who has not the pleasure to know you." We may indeed join with Miss Burney in admiring the " great sweetness and condescension of this speech. I was quite ashamed of this *apology,* but did not know what to say to it. But how amiable a simplicity in her speaking of herself, 'for one who has not the pleasure to know you.' " And she was by-and-by to have full experience of the queen's sweetness and condescension, who was often to address her in this gentle, deferential way.

Again, when the king remarked, " How time flies ! " the queen answered, " Oh, for me, I am always quarrelling with time ; it is so short to do something, and so long to do nothing."   " Time," broke in the king, "always seems long when we are young, and short when we begin to grow old."   " But nothing," added the queen, " makes me so angry as to hear people not know what to do. For me, I have never half time enough to do things. What makes me more angry still is to see people go up to a window and say, ' What a bad day, dear ! What shall we do such a day as this ? ' ' Do ? ' I say, 'why, employ yourselves, and then what signifies a bad day ? ' "   Here was shrewd sense and sagacity.

Reviewing this interesting interview, Miss Burney declared that the queen's manners had an easy dignity, with a most engaging simplicity, and that she had all "that fine high breeding which the mind, not the station gives, of carefully avoiding to distress those who converse with her. In her manner to the king, she made it appear that her study was to raise his consequence with others, by showing that she considers herself, though queen to the nation only, to him the first and most obedient of subjects."

It should be mentioned that there was an old-fashioned etiquette in receiving the king on his entrance. Miss Planta would go out walking backwards to fetch candles, which she brought in two at a time and distributed about the room. Next she served his Majesty with tea, offering a tray with a napkin over the arm. In other homes these were done by the mistress, but here Mrs. Delany was not supposed to attempt this duty.

A few days later there was another visit and another pleasant talk, when the queen asked her, "Miss Burney, have you heard that Boswell is going to publish a life of your friend Dr. Johnson? I tell you as I heard. I can't tell what he will do. He is so extraordinary a man, that perhaps he will devise something extraordinary." (How delighted would "Bozzy" have been had this speech been repeated, which we may be sure it never was.) She then began to discuss Madame de Genlis, whom she admired, and who sent her all her books. She talked of German literature, and complained that "they translate all our worst. And they write so finely now, even for the most silly books, that it makes one read on, and one cannot help it. Oh, I am very angry at that,"—she alluded to " The Sorrows of Werther"—"very finely writ, and I can't bear it." Speaking of another book, she astonished the listeners by saying that " she had picked it up *on a stall.*" "Oh, it is amazing what good books there are on stalls. Why, I don't pick them up myself, but I have a servant very clever ; and if they are not to be had at the book-sellers, are they not for me any more than for another ? "

She then gossiped on in a most agreeable way about Klopstock and Milton and the Catholics. " It is amusing, and pretty too, to see how sincere the lower people are of the Catholics "—which led to a little anecdote of her mother and herself when they were in a Catholic town.

" Once," she said, " I wanted to go to a chapel in that Catholic town, and my mother said I should if I would be sure not to laugh at anything. So I took care to keep my eyes half shut, half open ; this for fear I should see something to make me laugh. But there was nothing."

It was about this time that Mrs. Haggerdorn, who had come from Germany nearly thirty years before, and was Keeper of the Robes with Mrs. Schwellenberg, wished to return to her country. Her post became vacant, and the queen at once thought of the sprightly young novelist to succeed her. The engage-ment was made in the most delicate and encourag-ing way. She put no questions as to her qualifications,

but merely said, " with her most condescending softness,"
" I am sure, Miss Burney, we shall suit one another very
well ; " and another time, " I am sure we shall do very
well together." Naturally, there was general astonishment at this appointment, for the place had been sought
" by thousands of women of fashion and rank."

She entered on her duties at once, but nothing could
exceed the delicate conduct of the queen, who at first
allowed her to look on, so as to learn at her ease the general
routine. All the little glimpses of the royal family tell
the same tale of the quiet simplicity of the family. Thus
when she was at tea at Mrs. Schwellenberg's, and the
household was assembled, " the door opened and a young
lady entered, upon whose appearance *all the company rose
and retreated a few paces backward* with looks of high
respect. She desired that a basin of tea should be brought
to the music-room for Mrs. Delany. Then walking up
to me with a countenance of great sweetness, said, ' I
hope you are very well, Miss Burney.' " This was
Princess Elizabeth. It will be noted that she brought
the message for the tea herself.

The queen surrounded herself with a number of
persons pursuing literary tastes, and who filled some
trifling post in the household. These were chiefly
foreigners, and they are brought before us with much
graphic power by the lively Miss Burney. Among them
were Madame Lafitte, who read French to the queen,
Madame de Luc, Rev. de La Giffardière, and some
more.

In all this range of fiction there is nothing better than " Fanny's " sketch of this wild clergyman, and his frantic adoration. She had indeed succeeded in turning the heads of most of the household. She herself has written nothing so good as her talks with this cleric. He also read to the queen. This personage was a Prebendary of Winchester and minister of the French Chapel. He wrote a course of ancient history for his pupils, the English princesses, and which was dedicated to the queen and published under her good-natured patronage.[1] Madam de Luc's husband was an eminent mathematician; he invented a barometer, which he exhibited to their Majesties, who took the deepest interest in all inventions of the kind. In their regular practical fashion they patronized his instruments, and did something for his wife.

The queen's " readers," both of French and English, had no sinecures : even as her hair was being dressed, a long and tedious operation, some choice work was read to her. Miss Burney was once called upon to give a taste of her quality. Naturally, the queen and her daughters found a pleasure in anticipating the treat of an entertaining work being read aloud by a clever and sprightly writer. It, however, only furnished the incorrigible Fanny with an opportunity for displaying all her affectations ; she made a regular " business " of it.

Her Majesty was certainly a clever person, with a

[1] I possess a copy—with an inscription in her Majesty's handwriting —presented to Lord Sydney at Weymouth.

genuine taste for literature. She had her own favourite authors, whom she read with a steady appreciation. The most striking evidence of her cleverness is assuredly the extraordinary rapidity with which she acquired not merely a good knowledge of the English tongue, but a taste for English works. The Rev. Dr. Majendie, who instructed her, must have been astonished at her progress. As we have seen, she had also a great fancy for exercising herself in composition, and, as the king's festival came round, would present him with a little piece written for the occasion :—

SONG.

To peace and love, in courts but seldom seen,
This smiling day has sacred been ;
And may they here united reign,
While winter chills, or summer warms the plain !

May SHE, whose duty is her joy,
Still, still on tasks of love her hours employ,
To cheer her king—to charm her friend—
On his and Britain's hope with pleasure tend !

That lovely, that unfolding rose,
With care to watch, and cherish as he grows,
While, with a mother's soft surprise,
She sees in him renewed, his parent rise.

SECOND SONG.

Let harmony reign,
And let pleasure abound ;
While in sparkling champagne
This health goes around—
The king !—may his birthday successively smile,
With joy on himself, and with peace to his isle !
All white be his moments, and bear on their wing,
In the brightness of summer, the softness of spring !

May she, who bestowed him on Britain this morn,
Live long his mild sway to applaud and adorn!
May each loyal guest that around him is seen,
Embrace as his sister, whom love made his queen!
　　Then let harmony reign,
　　　And let pleasure abound,
　　While in sparkling champagne,
　　　These wishes go round.

She was often found reading such thoughtful works as
" The Observer," and would ask for the key to the names,
such as Vanessa, &c. She recognized Hume under his
fictitious name. When Mr. Bolton came to teach her
children geography, she would seize the opportunity to
get a private lesson herself, as the master would stand
before her, book in hand, expounding his craft. In fact,
no master came to give them lessons from whom she did
not get some instruction save the professor of dancing.
This was extraordinary.

The scene at "the walking on the Terrace"—always a
pretty and effective one—never seemed to lack attraction for the lieges of the palace. It had a deep signifi-
cance, for it brought the royal family into close contact
with their subjects. On one birthday in 1786, the
centre of all eyes was the little Princess Amelia—an
interesting, affectionate creature, cut off in an untimely
way—who walked in front by herself, dressed in a robe
coat and a close-fitting cap, with fan and gloves. She
was enchanted with everything, turning from side to
side to see every one. There was a regular lane formed,
many deep—all the "Terracers," as they were called,
being packed against the wall, but straining forward to

get notice from the royal party. Many journeyed from London when they wanted to freshen or keep alive the royal memory. When the queen and king recognized any one, there was a bow and a smile, or a regular stop, and a lively conversation ensued; then the party moved forward. When these persons were passed a second time, the recognition was renewed. So every faculty of the royal pair was kept on the stretch. The train was a long one—the Princess Royal leaning on Lady Walde-grave, and Princess Augusta with the Duchess of Ancaster.

When Mrs. Thrale's collection of Johnson's letters came out, they were eagerly read at the palace. Nothing better shows the queen's interest in literary matters than her keen appreciation of the volumes, and her judicious criticisms. It was no mere superficial talk over a new book ; there was, no doubt, an additional piquancy from the fact that one of her ladies was indirectly concerned. The Bishop of Carlisle had a copy which he lent to the queen's reader, " Mr. Turbulent," and which was lent by him to her Majesty. It seems odd that the new books did not find their way directly to the royal hands, but there was a thrifty spirit regulating these matters, and we know that the queen would even send her maid to purchase a book at a stall. The letters passed on to Mrs. Schwellenberg, who was hardly likely to appreciate them, and who in her turn lent them to Fanny. The queen read them " with the utmost avidity," and she was naturally eager to know all

about the allusions and suppressed names. She pressed
Mrs. Schwellenberg on the matter before Miss Burney.
" No, I have them yet to read," was the answer.   The
queen said they were most interesting for the public at
large : then the Schwellenberg, recalling that Fanny had
been " chaffed " about them, said, " Your Majesty will
hurt Miss Burney ; yesterday it had driven her out of
the room."   The queen, who was singularly delicate in
such matters, and had purposely avoided appealing to
Fanny, lest she might be distressed—the heroine
absurdly fancying that she was the subject of the general
talk—took occasion, when they were alone, to say,
" with her softest manner," and looking her earnestly
in the face, " You could not be offended at what I
said ? "   With due affectation she answered that she
was longing to speak to the queen on the matter, but
could not delay to express her sense of the *levity*
with which the matter had been treated in her hearing.
The queen said that she knew she had always spoken as
little as she could of the affair, but the letters had better
been spared the printing.   She wished that Mr. Langton,
Dr. Johnson's friend, would publish his notes (Langton
gave them to Mr. Boswell).   " But," added her Majesty,
" I think Dr. Johnson wanted one friend more."
" What for, madam ? "   " *A friend to suppress them !* "
What an idea this gives us of the queen's tranquil and
unaffected criticism !

Miss Burney's sketches of the equerries and gentle-
men-in-waiting are perfect portraits and admirably done
—the languid *dilettante* flirt, Colonel " Fairly "; Colonel

Budè; the pleasant, careless Colonel Manners, who said " everything that came into his head."

This Colonel Manners was always exhibiting his gay, *insouciant* ways—his free criticisms and careless indifference to the royalties and his duties. He must have been a charming fellow. When the crisis came he was to show himself a trusty and devoted partisan of the court, ready to risk his life in the cause. He would speak coolly of the court—" Of course I shall go to Ascot : it is my turn of duty ; *I think it right to be civil to the king.*" He would ridicule Herschel and his wonderful discoveries —" I liked him well enough till he came to his volcanoes in the moon, then I gave him up." Discussing antique dress, he gravely said, " Why, you may wear things of all times, ever so far back—*even the buckles of four years ago—* if you wish." This is delightful. He persisted in joining in the music at church, though he could not make a note, sometimes " running into ' God save the King.' " [1] But his perpetual rallying of the Schwellenberg was a rich entertainment for them all.[2]

Once the flighty lady-in-waiting went off for a walk with Mr. Smelt, having heard that the " Royalties " had gone to Windsor. She returned leisurely, and was walking up-

---

[1] It was of him that the Schwellenberg put the droll question, " Colonel Manners, he sleep wid you ? He sleep wid me sometimes."

[2] On one occasion he announced that he had found in his bed a great greasy lump of leather which she had placed there. The poor lady screamed out at the charge, " I know noding from your ledder for your bed."—" Well, your maid does," he went on coolly, " my man found it there.—' Shovel it out,' I said.—' It's Madame Schwellenberg,' he said, ' here's her name on it.'—' Well, sell it to-morrow to the saddlers ! ' "

stairs when she encountered Princess Amelia and Mrs.
Cheveley, who told her that the queen had been sending
for her. Filled with consternation, she rushed to her
Majesty, and found her under the hairdressers, her
daughters and several noble dames attending. The foolish young woman "stood in the door confused," as well
she might be, for the queen said, not a little dryly,
" Where have you been, Miss Burney ? " She told her
story—the good-humoured lady once more passed it over,
and good-naturedly bade her look at some dress, and say
if it were not pretty.

Once she was called upon to read aloud to the queen
and court :—

" The moment coffee was over, the Princess Elizabeth
came for me. I found her Majesty knotting, the Princess
Royal drawing, Princess Augusta spinning, and Lady
Courtown, I believe, in the same employment, but I saw
none of them perfectly well.

" ' Come, Miss Burney,' cried the queen, ' how are
your spirits ?—How is your voice ? '—' She says,
ma'am,' cried the kind Princess Elizabeth, ' she shall do
her best.' This had been said in attending her Royal
Highness back. I could only confirm it, and that *cheerfully* — to hide *fearfully.*

" I had not the advantage of choosing my play, nor do I
know what would have been my decision had it fallen to
my lot. Her Majesty had just begun Colman's works,
and ' Polly Honeycomb ' was to open my campaign.
' I think,' cried the queen most graciously, ' Miss

Burney will read the better for drawing a chair and
sitting down.'—' O yes, mamma! I dare say so!' cried
Princess Augusta and Princess Elizabeth, both in a
moment.

" The queen then told me to draw my chair close to her
side. I made no scruples. Heaven knows I needed not
the addition of standing! but most glad I felt in being
placed thus near, as it saved a constant painful effort of
loud reading.

" ' Lady Courtown,' cried the queen, 'you had better
draw nearer, for Miss Burney *has the misfortune* of reading
rather low at first.'

" Nothing could be more amiable than this opening.
Accordingly, I did, as I had promised, my best; and
indifferent as that was, it would rather have surprised
you, all things considered, that it was not yet worse.
But I exerted all the courage I possess, and, having often
read to the queen, I felt how much it behoved me not to
let her surmise I had any *greater* awe to surmount. It is
but a vulgar performance; and I was obliged to omit, as
well as I could at sight, several circumstances very unpleasant for reading, and ill enough fitted for such
hearers. It went off pretty flat. Nobody is to comment,
nobody is to interrupt; and even between one act and
another not a moment's pause is expected to be made.
I had been already informed of this etiquette by Mr.
Turbulent and Miss Planta; nevertheless, it is not only
oppressive to the reader, but loses to the hearers so much
spirit and satisfaction, that I determined to endeavour,

should I again be called upon, to introduce a little break into this tiresome and unnatural profundity of respectful solemnity.   My own embarrassment, however, made it agree with me, for the present, uncommonly well.   Lady Courtown never uttered one single word the whole time ; yet is she one of the most loquacious of our establishment.   But such is the settled etiquette.

"The queen has a taste for conversation, and the princesses a good-humoured love for it, that doubles the regret of such an annihilation of all nature and all pleasantry.   But what will not prejudice and education inculcate ?   They have been brought up to annex silence to respect and decorum : to talk, therefore, unbid, or to differ from any given opinion, even when called upon, are regarded as high improprieties, if not presumptions. They none of them do justice to their own minds, while they enforce this subjection upon the minds of others. I had not experienced it before ; for when reading alone with the queen, or listening to her reading to me, I have always frankly spoken almost whatever has occurred to me.   But there I had no other examples before me, and therefore I might inoffensively be guided by myself ; and her Majesty's continuance of the same honour has shown no disapprobation of my proceeding.   But here it was not easy to make any decision for myself ; to have done what Lady Courtown forbore doing would have been undoubtedly a liberty.

" So we all behaved alike ; and easily can I now conceive the disappointment and mortification of poor Mr.

Garrick when he read 'Lethe' to a royal audience.   Its
tameness must have tamed him, and I doubt not he
never acquitted himself so ill."

The volatile Burney found it hard to fall in with the
almost conventual rules of the establishment, and almost
at once began to try the patience of her tolerant mistress.
It was extraordinary what freedoms she indulged herself in.
Once the queen bade her go and take a walk for her
health's sake.   She went off to see Madame Lafitte, who
detained her with gossips, &c., until she was too late
for her noon attendance.   She had not time to dress
properly, and slipped on a morning gown and large cap.
The queen was preparing to have her hair dressed, and was
left without an attendant.   But the good-natured lady only
said with a smile, " Now, Miss Burney, you may go back
and finish your dressing."   This hairdressing, powdering,
&c., which was indispensable, must have been an intolerable burden ; it was a serious, elaborate business, required
the services of a hairdresser, and took an immense time.
The ladies naturally found it difficult to secure the
services of a *friseur*.   There was a bell which was rung
in the queen's room when Fanny's services were required : a method of summons which the young lady
resented, as suggesting ringing for a servant.

The ceremonial on the queen's retiring for the night
was always formal, and strictly regulated.   Her Majesty
was " handed into her dressing-room " by the king, Mrs.
Schwellenberg being in attendance, the two princesses
following whose quarters were at the queen's lodge;

the "lower lodge" being for the younger princesses. Then the king kissed his daughters, who with due respect kissed their mother's hand, wished her good-night, and withdrew. The admirable royal lady was always up before seven, and her ladies had to rise at six ; she then put on her hat and a simple morning gown and cloak and took her way to the chapel for morning prayers.

Among her attendants were the two Ladies Walde-grave, who having been left orphans, were considerately given places and taken under her Majesty's care. Lady Elizabeth was lady of the bedchamber to the Princess Royal. Lady Charlotte Finch, an old and well-tried servant, did very well for her family, having her three daughters, including a married one, Mrs. Fielding, established at court. Miss Goldsworthy, the sub-gover-ness known as "Gooley," Miss Planta, and a whole cohort of readers, were useful assistants : indeed her royal daughters required a large number of lady attendants.

On court days, the queen dressed her head at Kew and drove into London ; but on the more important drawing-room days this was done at St. James's Palace. There was a regular etiquette here in her dressing. One of her bedchamber women helped the queen to dress ; Mrs. Fielding attached her necklace, handed her fan and gloves ; the others held up her train.

The queen's indulgence to Fanny was particularly shown in the matters of the numerous petitions which the injudicious young lady insisted in presenting directly to her Majesty in behalf of friends and relations. This was against all rule and etiquette, as such things should come though the hands of secretaries and proper officials. At last her Majesty had to tell her that she must desist from the practice, adding gently, that it was the fact that of the many she had brought to her not one had the least claim to consideration.

Surrounded as she was by such a number of courtiers and dependents, whose interests were opposed, the queen naturally felt she lived in an atmosphere of whisperings and intrigue, where it was difficult to reach the truth. A slight incident might rouse her suspicions. Of this an amusing instance occurred when " Colonel Fairly," having learned that the head of St. Catherine's, Mr. Marsh, had died, wrote the news to Miss Burney, with the view that the queen might have the news as early as possible. This was hardly as thoughtful a step as it appeared, for he was looking for the place himself. Instead of telling her royal mistress herself, Miss Burney told the news to another, who was to communicate it to the queen. No doubt she wished to conceal this mark of Colonel Fairly's confidence, for their flirtation was already the subject of the court gossip. It is evidence of the queen's sagacity that she thought these little chicaneries suspicious, or at least not straightforward, and at once proceeded to trace the story to its source, saying she thought it most singular that the news had not been communicated to her by the person who received it. Miss Burney had to acknowledge that she was the recipient. The letter had to be produced, as the queen put some questions showing her distrust, and the whole had rather an awkward appearance of concealment. When all was cleared up, her Majesty gave away the place to " Colonel Fairly," who had asked for it.

CHAPTER VIII.

THE KING'S ILLNESS.

LADY HARCOURT, daughter-in-law of the Lord Harcourt who some five-and-twenty years before had been despatched to Strelitz to arrange the marriage, had always continued on terms of the most affectionate intimacy with the queen. She was one of her ladies, and to her the queen unbosomed her thoughts and feelings in the most confidential way; for no family, as we have said, did the royal pair show such an unbounded affection. At Nuneham, near Oxford, are preserved some hundreds of letters from the king [1] and queen and princesses, all written in a strain of engaging familiarity and confidence ; full, too, of a pleasant gaiety and enjoyment, and the intimacy is creditable to the merits of the family that was thus distinguished. From this long friendship with her royal mistress, Lady Harcourt was able to form a true and faithful estimate of her

---

[1] The late Mr. Vernon Harcourt printed these private papers in a number of very interesting volumes, which form a record of intimate court life that can scarcely be equalled for interest or for entertainment. He was kind enough to present me with one of the volumes, and allowed me to use the work as it suited my purpose.

character, and she has left a somewhat elaborate estimate
of the queen, which even as a piece of literary work, and
psychological appreciation, has high merit.   I give it here
at length.

" Her understanding," she says, " was indeed of the
first class; it was equally quick and solid—she tasted wit
in others, but checked it in herself, from being aware
that dangerous as it is in all situations, it would be
particularly so in hers.   Her mind was highly cultivated,
she was fond of reading, and well acquainted with the
best authors—English, German, and French—and her
memory was so retentive that she never forgot what she
once knew.   In the talent of conversing she had few
equals; whether the subject was serious or lively, she
treated it in such a manner that those must have been
very stupid indeed who did not listen to her with
pleasure; no one narrated better than she did, and
anecdotes that had little merit themselves were made
interesting in the way she told them.   There was a
sweetness in her manner and an animation of countenance which caused many who thought her plain before
they conversed with her to admire her afterwards.   She
certainly had no pretensions to beauty, but her hair and
teeth were fine, and her eyes expressive.   She was not
tall, but her figure was good, and her manners remarkably graceful.   She   understood music, and had a
pleasing voice; she had a decided genius for drawing,
which, if that art had been cultivated by her in early
years, would have enabled her to excel in it.   She was

strict and sincere in her religious duties, and her love
of truth was unbounded. She hated flattery, and
despised those who practised it. She was very sensitive,
but always seemed to restrain her feelings from
principle. Her unknown charities were extensive, and
to those about her she was endeared by little delicate
attentions by which she seemed always striving to give
them pleasure. Her confidence she imparted to few,
from a strong fear lest she should be suspected of
favouritism. She judged characters quickly and truly,
and her warm heart was truly attached to those who she
felt loved the individual as much as they respected the
queen. I remember once saying to her, 'I should like
to tell you something, but pray promise never to let the
queen know it.' She laughed, and said, 'Oh, no, *she*
can have no business with what passes between us in our
private unreserved conversations.' So it was always
with those who shared her private hours. She then
conversed with freedom, wishing them to do the same,
and entered into all their concerns with affectionate
interest."

This presents a very charming, even engaging form
of character. It brings with it, too, proportionate conviction of truth, for it is consistent.

This confidential attendant of the queen's had been, in
1784, appointed Lady of the Bedchamber, and, from
that time to her death, was regarded by the royal
family with feelings of the tenderest attachment—an
attachment that more or less extended to Archbishop

Harcourt and other members of the family. To her the queen addressed the most confidential of letters—full also of a pleasant gaiety, and even playfulness. To this devoted and sympathizing friend she disclosed her thoughts with the utmost freedom. The best testimony to the sterling worth, simple affectionate nature of the queen and her daughters is found in the letters of condolence addressed by the family to her on the loss of Lord Harcourt, and to her family on her own demise.

Happy had been this excellent queen, had only these little worries of the court been her lot. But now, weighty and serious trials were impending. They indeed seemed destined to await her and her family in a regular series, coming " in battalions," as it were. These always seemed to take an unusual and out-of-the-way form of affliction.

The symptoms and the distressing stages of the king's malady in 1788 have been often described. A more painful episode, a more embarrassing situation, or one more charged with tragic horrors cannot be imagined; and though private families have often had to endure this most painful and trying of all afflictions, it may be said that nothing in this way approached the complications and miseries the royal family had to pass through. There was the severity of the attack, the high position of the victim, the general publicity, the unseemly contest that raged round him, the opposing interests of the queen and princes, the difficulties of applying proper restraint, the band of contending doctors, the greed and animosity of the contending factions— elements that all joined to make a scene of intense misery and horror. Perhaps the greatest sufferer was the unhappy queen herself, who, ill in mind and body, found every night and day a time of agony.

On the eve of the crisis there was a sense of impending horror, and the queen seemed a prey to a secret terror. There were violent bursts of tears, with much walking up and down the room, shaking of her head in irresolution and distress. Still the king went about as usual—would drive out in his chaise. How agitated the queen was, was shown by her anger at a paragraph in a morning paper, when she declared it should be brought to account ; she then burnt it.

This excellent and amiable lady, then, after more than twenty years of sunshine, had now to call on all her resources of character to encounter a series of miseries, which day by day seemed to grow in their intensity. Lady Harcourt traces minutely for us the various stages of the king's malady. It seems to have begun on June 11th, 1788, with a bilious fever, from which the king recovered. The Cheltenham waters, which he had drunk too profusely, were supposed to be the cause of his malady. A rash came out over his face, which seems to have been driven in. He was particularly careless as to getting wet, changing his clothes, &c., and it was once noticed how the water actually ran out of his boots " when he took them off." Still, he went through his levées and such functions ; but when the family returned to Windsor, all were struck with his shrunk, haggard face. He said on entering, "I return to you a poor old man, weak in mind and body." Sunday, the 26th, was the first fatal day on which the malady regularly declared itself. In the middle of the sermon in church, he suddenly started up, and embraced the queen and princesses in a rather frantic way, saying, "You know what it is to be nervous." Fortunately this could not be seen by the congregation. The doctors were called in—Heberden and Sir G. Baker—who ordered him a blister on his head. But he did not mend. His family were now infinitely disturbed by a rapidity of talk or "gabble," and his eyes, as the queen said, had become "like black currant jelly," the veins in his face all swelled, and the sound of his voice dreadful. "She described his talking on and on till he had to stop from actual exhaustion, but the instant he recovered breath, he began until the foam ran out of his mouth." These were the dreadful "hurries" which filled his family with such terror, and which were to be the chief "note" of his mania. He actually talked his voice away altogether.

About October 25th, the royal party, which had put off their migration to Windsor, was able to set forth, there being an improvement in the king's state. But the queen showed yet more and more uneasiness. She would distract herself by reading instructive books, such as Hunter on the New Testament ; but when she came to a touching passage would break down. "How nervous I am," she would cry. "I am quite a fool—don't you think so?" "No, ma'am," was her retainer's plain reply.

There was one dreadful scene at the dinner-table on November 5th, when the violence of the malady first declared itself, which was long remembered. The prince was so affected as to be near fainting; one of the princesses had to rub his forehead with Hungary water, and he had to be "blooded." The queen fell into violent hysterics. Lady Harcourt does not mention what occurred, but long after, at Lord Jersey's table, the prince described the scene. The king suddenly rose, caught his son by the collar and pushed him against the wall with some violence, asking him who would dare to say to the king of England that he should not speak out, or who should prevent his whispering? He then whispered.[1] It is plain that the prince had incautiously tried to restrain him and keep him quiet. His womanish terror and alarm at the attack showed that there was ground for the king's repeated declaration that there was only one of his family that lacked personal courage. After this painful scene the queen, as soon as it was possible, got away—she had put a constraint upon herself, Lady Harcourt says, " beyond what she had strength to support, and as soon as she got into her room, she had an hysterical fit. Lady G. Waldegrave was the only person with her, but they were soon joined by the king, who, upon the lady telling him that the queen was ill, said, ' Then I will take care of her myself.' The queen made Lady Ely a sign not to leave her, and presently

[1] Mr. Jesse quotes the account from the unpublished Willis MS.

the king proposed removing her Majesty into the drawing-room, when he made a sort of bed upon one of the sofas and placed her on it. He then fixed where each of the princesses should sit, and ordered all the candles except two to be put out." It was hinted to him that her Majesty should have a separate room : he agreed on condition that his should be next hers, but it was not until past midnight that he could be induced to let the queen go to her room.

Nothing is more dramatically vivid than Miss Burney's descriptions of these terrible scenes. All that night she sat in her room, alone, and a prey to impending terrors. There was a mysterious silence abroad. She would open her door to listen; not even the sound of a servant passing could be heard.[1]

At last the queen sent for her. "I could hardly get along—hardly force myself into her room—dizzy I felt almost to falling." Fanny was not likely to be of much practical use. "My poor royal mistress! Never can I forget her countenance—pale, ghastly pale, she looked. She was seated to be undressed : her whole frame was disordered, yet she was still and quiet. Her two ladies assisted me to undress her, or rather I assisted them, for they were firmer from being longer present, my shaking hands and blinded eyes could scarce be of

---

[1] "We were now alone. But I could not speak, neither did Mr. Fairly. I had begun a hassock. If I had not had my work, I must have left the room to quiet myself." It is characteristic to find that previously she had found opportunity for indulgence in a little quiet "flirtation" with her Colonel "**Fairly**"—or Colonel Digby.

any use." So we could fancy. She gave her some camphor julep. "'How cold I am!' she cried, and put her hand on mine: marble it felt." The king, as we saw, had insisted on being near at hand, so a bed was put up for him in the queen's second dressing-room. Miss Goldsworthy was to sit up with her poor lady.

A terrible night, that of November 6th, often described, was to follow. Miss Burney offered to sit up, but the queen would only have her own maids. "How reluctantly I came away!" says Fanny, "how hardly to myself leave her! Yet I went to bed, determined to preserve my strength to the utmost of my ability for the service of my unhappy mistress. She rose at six." She tells all that follows dramatically. She rose early, stole along the passages and found that everyone— attendants, pages and all—had sat up the whole night: the king's state was so alarming. His sudden entry on the party of watchers, and Colonel Digby's courageous attempt to get him back to his bed, is well described by Miss Burney. She found the hapless queen sitting up in bed. "Miss Burney, how are you?" she faltered; then burst into a torrent of weeping, which she did not check. Then came her pathetic speech, "*I thank you, Miss Burney—you have made me cry.* It is a great relief to me. I had not been able to cry before, all this night long." During this time the distraught king was heard in the next room talking unceasingly, and attended by two doctors—an element of horror in the situation, enough to drive the poor lady out of her wits.

" During the night, about one o'clock, he came into her room, took up her light, held it to her face, and said, ' Yes, I am not deceived : I thought she was here ; I thought she would not leave me.' He turned to Miss Goldsworthy and said, ' Goully, you are honest, you will take care of the queen.' He then put down the light and walked fast about the room. The queen implored him to go and take some rest, when he left the room, shutting the door with violence and locking it."

Sir George Baker, to whom the king was accustomed, appears to have been a poor timorous creature, and on this occasion completely shrank from his duties, apparently intimidated by the prince. While still partly sane the king had called him " an old woman." The queen, who thought she could rely on him, summoned him, but he pleaded that he was "in a violent perspiration," &c., and would not come, on which the prince sent for another " leech."

There now appeared on the scene a rather striking and masterful figure, that of Dr. Warren, the fashionable physician of the day. A clever, ambitious man, persuasive, and devoted to the faction on whose side he had placed himself. When it is said that he represented *medically* the prince's interests during this tragic episode, and was employed to hold as suspicious, to check, and frustrate if possible, every move in the game made by the queen and her supporters, it may be imagined what confusion and unseemly struggles were likely to arise. All through these miseries his rather ill-omened figure is seen hovering about: the whisper that "Dr. Warren was arrived" struck a chill to the heart of the queen. With him it was that the royal lady had to do constant battle in defence of all that was dearest to her, and it must be said that she bore herself with undaunted courage. The king had a particular dislike to him.

Lady Harcourt sketches him more minutely. He had, she says, a strong understanding—a dictatorial and supercilious manner, "with that sort of inflexible firmness that is rarely found with a feeling heart. He was a master of dissimulation. He was most acceptable to titled families; with them his brow unbent: he became gay and lively, and to his lady patients would recommend dissipation and amusement, as health, he said, depended on the spirits. It was said, indeed, that he lent them money." Such a man was exactly suited to the purposes of the Prince of Wales.

He arrived promptly—declared at once that "the king was in the greatest danger, and that serious measures should be taken." No doubt this was correct enough, and it exactly met the views of the prince. But almost at once the poor queen was to discover what bold attempts would be made to set her aside, and thus frustrate her efforts to protect her husband. Now was to begin the reckless and unscrupulous attacks to gain control of his person, and the power of deciding whether he was fit to resume his power. The prince and his faction were the unscrupulous leaders of this conspiracy : though due allowance must be made for the heat of party, and for the natural persuasion that the queen and her faction would strain everything to represent the king as restored to reason. It must be admitted that the interests on both sides in the condition of the king were about equal, and also vital ; and the likelihood of being blinded by prejudice and by the persuasion of the wickedness of their opponents lay as much on one side as on the other. But still the situation of the prince and his party was well-nigh desperate : it was felt that such an opportunity was not likely to occur again. And thus the extraordinary and unedifying battle between mother and son began.

The queen, who of course saw more of him than any one else, seemed to have divined, with a dismal foreboding, all that was coming ; and everyone noticed her expression and uneasy looks.

Word was brought to her that Dr. Warren (who had been sent for in the middle of the night) was now "observing" the king, and listening, from another room, for his patient had positively refused to see him. He heard all his ravings. The poor queen, in an agony of expectation and anxiety, was ordered to keep her bed —as an excuse for not going to the patient, who was ceaselessly calling for her. A strange terror of him had seized upon her. He was indeed only next door. She constantly made her ladies listen and report what he was saying. Then she thought of having her prayers read out, or a sermon, but could not fix her thoughts. She declared she could see no one in this dreadful state, "expecting every moment to be broke in upon." She was feverishly anxious to see Warren on this point and get official direction for "keeping away." So she waited and waited long. But there was no sign of Dr. Warren. She sent for Baker. He could not, he said, see her alone. Then for Hawkins, the palace doctor, who referred her to Dr. Warren. In this cruel state her ladies implored her to remove to another room at a distance, where she would not hear the king's ravings; but they could not prevail. She rose and sat in her nightdress in the adjoining dressing-room to await Dr. Warren and his advice.

"Presently came news that Warren had quitted his post of watching, and now the poor queen with a torrent of tears prepared to see him. She waited and waited, but he came not. All astonished and impatient, she despatched one of the Waldegrave ladies to make inquiries. He was gone! Gone without even noticing her request! 'Run! stop him! Let him tell me what to do!'" But he did not come. This was significant. He was completely under the direction of the prince, and no attention was now to be paid to the poor lady's wishes.

"A deeper blow I never witnessed," says Miss Burney. All the attention showed her was an official direction from the doctors that she was to move to another room at once. Two poor apartments were found for the queen of England—a bedroom and a sitting-room—and one for her lady-in-waiting. She went without a murmur; but arrived there, fell into an agony of grief, uttering frenzied lamentations—"What will become of me ? " These are truly distressing scenes, and as dramatic as they are distressing.

Now came a dreadful business. The doctors had declared that the king must be removed to Kew, so as to be away from the bustle and publicity of Windsor Castle. Dr. Willis, the clergyman-physician, who was pronounced to have great success in dealing with lunacy, had been called in ; but the prince affected to consider him the queen's creature, and was loud in his abuse of him. The doctors were indeed divided into factions. Henceforth, therefore, there was to be an indecent conflict going on, in which there was not so much thought of the hapless victim, as of the political interests of those who were contending.

The first issue joined was on this point of removal. The prince and his friends, in very rough and overbearing fashion, insisted that the queen, the king's sole protectress, should not be with him. Her son tried to force her to go to the " Queen's House " in London, or else to remain at Windsor. But she was altogether against the removal, and remonstrated firmly. The prince said that " he was resolved upon it," and that the ministers approved, and that she must be separated from the king—on which, as Lady Harcourt relates, the fearless lady said to him, " *Prince of Wales, do it at your peril ! Where the king is, there shall I be.*" And the brave woman prevailed.

With much contrivance and difficulty the king was got into the carriage, the inducement being that he was going to see the queen. The royal party had gone on before, and nervously waited his arrival, not knowing what might happen. For the poor daughters we must have the deepest sympathy. They had to control their own feelings and miseries, to strive and soothe their unhappy mother, who henceforth continued in the most wretched condition, in one perpetual stream of tears.

The incident of this removal to Kew was another agony for the queen. She set off from her room, at the moment she was directed to do, glided along the passage and got into the waiting carriage, attended by the weeping daughters and the faithful Lady Courtown. The third princess and Lady C. Finch followed. There was no state or parade ; it was as though going to an execution. But there was not a dry eye in the household. All the footmen, housemaids, the porter, sentinels, all cried abundantly as they moved on. The three younger princesses were to wait until news came how matters had gone off.

At Kew there was an agony of suspense, and a miserable uncertainty as to the success of the scheme. Messengers would arrive to report progress. At last it became known that he had been successfully got off and was now on his way.

The prince, who had assumed the whole direction of the situation, had ridden over to Kew beforehand, had gone over the palace arranging and allotting all the rooms, marking the names on the doors with his own hand. There was but scant accommodation, and the ladies had to put up with servants' accommodation. The poor queen was treated unceremoniously and given an ordinary bedroom and drawing-room, for her proper rooms were over the king's, and these were now locked for fear of his being disturbed. As the moment drew on for the departure, the mystery at Windsor increased. Everywhere, in the passages, were the doctors, the prince and his friends, consulting as to how the king was to be tempted away. It was a critical operation, and all the time the unhappy monarch, shut up in his room, could be heard pouring forth his torrent of talk and calling for the queen.

At Kew, after an interval, which Miss Burney filled up with a lively flirtation with Colonel Digby, "dinner went on, and still no king. We now began to grow very anxious, when Miss Planta exclaimed that she thought she heard a carriage. We all listened. 'I hope!' I cried. 'I see you do!' cried he; 'you have a very face of hope at this moment!'—and it was not disappointed. The sound came nearer, and presently a carriage drove into the front court. I could see nothing, it was so dark; but I presently heard the much-respected voice of the dear unhappy king, speaking rapidly to the porter, as he alighted from the coach. Mr. Fairly flew instantly upstairs, to acquaint the queen with the welcome tidings. The poor king had been prevailed upon to quit Windsor with the utmost difficulty: he was accompanied by General Harcourt, his aide-de-camp, and Colonels Goldsworthy and Welbred—no one else! He had passed all the rest with apparent composure, to come to his carriage, for they lined the passage, eager to see him once more! and almost all Windsor was collected round the rails, &c., to witness the mournful spectacle of his departure, which left them in the deepest despondence, with scarce a ray of hope ever to see him again. The bribery, however, which brought him, was denied him!—he was by no means to see the queen! When I went to her at night she was all graciousness, and kept me till very late. I had not seen her alone so long, except for a few minutes in the morning, that I had a thousand things I wished to say to her. You may be sure they were all, as far as they went, consolatory. Princess Augusta had a small tent-bed put up in the queen's bed-chamber : I called her royal highness when the queen dismissed me. She undressed in an adjoining apartment." And so that agitating day came to a close.

CHAPTER IX.

WITH the change things now began to mend a little.
The queen and her daughters began to settle down.
The irrepressible Fanny amused herself by violent
quarrels with the Schwellenberg, by constant grumbling
at her accommodation.

In the midst of the horrors, when no one scarcely
slept, the volatile Fanny was carrying on her
flirtation with the staid widower, Colonel Digby.
Discipline was relaxed ; in the agitation of the times
everyone could do much as they pleased. The Colonel
was constantly coming to her to talk over matters in a
sorrowful way. The Schwellenberg went away. He
would offer himself to dine with her and Miss Planta,
two admiring ladies, and brought with him his little son.

" What a relief is this," he would say, " to dine thus
quietly."

But almost before the dessert was removed the
terrible lady appeared, and the party fled. " My reception was such as to make me deem it most proper again
to return to my room." Her return to duty rather
checked the flirtation, the Schwellenberg being ill and

in bad humour, " all spasm and horror," and announced
that nothing must be talked of. Mr. Fairly dropped
in constantly to read Cowper's " Task" to her !

The doctors were now coming and going. Sir L.
Pepys was a new one. Poor Miss Goldsworthy was
seriously laid up with illness from her labours, the
queen was crushed down with her affliction, but the
flirtation went on, and to Fanny's satisfaction was actually
talked of. Thus the weary days at Kew sped by,
everyone waiting and hoping for the time to come
which never came. The painful moment was in the
morning, when the point was to learn what sort of a
night the king had passed. The poor queen would send
out all her emissaries to gather up what they could—a
difficult matter, as a sort of mystery was kept up, and
nothing was to be told without leave of the prince, or
until the doctors came and settled the bulletin. When
things were very bad, there was the difficulty of soften-
ing the report, for the queen's sake. Then there was
the sickening disagreements of the mediciners, and the
growth of faction, all raging in the palace; no one
trusting the other persons in authority, insisting on
their right to see the sufferer and satisfy their suspicions,
and their claims being resisted or conceded ; with the
hurrying up to town to propagate the news.[1]

---

[1] These reports became often so contradictory and perplexing that
the agitated queen decreed that no one but Miss Burney should bring
them. That young lady would interrogate Mr. Hawkins, who, after
communicating something shocking, would add, " But you needn't tell
that to the queen."

This slight of the queen's not being allowed to see the physicians was the beginning of a new system introduced by the prince.   At first he had been tolerably considerate and affectionate ; but letters and messages had come to him from his political friends in town, evidently urging him to take command of the situation—and there were great political possibilities in view, which were to be turned to profit, and at once. Accordingly he now became master of the house, issuing his directions and commands ; no one was to be admitted without his leave ; faithful servants of the king were turned from the door, and the queen found that she was not to be considered at all, and must obey like the rest. The doctors took their cue from him, and were careless, as we have seen, as to her wishes and requests.

It was found, presently, that the behaviour of the royal pages was going beyond bounds, and the doctors agreed that they should be got rid of altogether. They were acting as spies. This dismissal was owing to the firmness of Dr. Willis, who, supported from outside by the feeling of the country, was fast gaining ground and carrying out whatever he had set his mind upon. The disgust of the faction at this removal of the pages was unconcealed, for it appeared that they depended on these people for information.

The Duke of Cumberland, Lady Harcourt wrote, let out at his own house that they found the page Ernest, the man they most depended on, he was their *steady* one, but that latterly his handwriting was so known that he got another to direct his letters, unless he could give them unseen to Warren. The Duke of Cumberland also candidly complained that the removal of the pages was " the most d—d measure that had ever been thought of, for now they did not know half so much of what was going on, and were obliged to depend on the physicians alone ; that d—d old fellow Willis was always with the king, and prevented Warren from getting him to himself, but that he was resolved he should see the king *alone* in spite of you all."

It should be said, however, that the animosities on both sides were so inflamed, and Lady Harcourt in particular so devoted a partisan of her royal mistress, that no doubt many of these stories were mere rumours or exaggerations. The cue was to make the opposing faction as black as possible.

At Kew, however, there began to be noted signs of improvement, with, however, many relapses. This was certainly owing to the treatment of the experienced Dr. Willis, who was a professional and experienced " mad doctor," as it is called, and who from the first all but guaranteed a cure. It was indeed only natural that such a person should know more of the business than the others ; and it was this knowledge and boldness that furnished the queen an admirable support and finally led her to victory. There can be no doubt that by this aid of Willis's and by her own undaunted spirit she was enabled to protect the unfortunate king throughout, and save him from being overwhelmed by an unscrupulous party.   It was a triumph, certainly, for a faithful wife.

Presently came that wonderful adventure which made Miss Burney the heroine of the hour, viz. her being chased by the distraught king round the garden and caught by him, when he detained her long, the doctors watching warily from a distance.

" I went very soon after to the queen ; I was most eager to avow the meeting, and how little I could help it.   Her astonishment, and her earnestness to hear every particular, were very great.   I told her almost all.   Some few things relating to the distressing questions I could not repeat ; nor many things said of Mrs. Schwellenberg, which would much, and very needlessly, have hurt her.   This interview, and the circumstances belonging to it, excited general curiosity, and all the house watched for opportunities to beg a relation of it.   How delighted was I to tell them all my happy prognostics ! "

The king was now gradually mending, and his harassed family was enabled to resume some at least of their tranquil pursuits.   " Two of the princesses regularly, and in turn, attend their royal mother in her evening visits to the king.   Some of those who stay behind now and then spend the time in Mrs. Schwellenberg's room. They all long for their turn of going to the king, and count the hours till it returns.   Their dutiful affection is truly beautiful to behold.

" This evening the Princesses Elizabeth and Mary came into Mrs. Schwellenberg's room while I was yet there.

They sang songs in two parts all the evening, and very prettily in point of voice. Their good humour, however, and inherent condescension and sweetness of manners, would make a much worse performance pleasing."

Fortunately, Willis, as the controlling power, was entitled to judge of the king's daily condition and to settle the bulletins. On this matter there was a perpetual conflict going on. On one critical occasion matters came to a crisis, Warren declaring that the bulletin did not correctly describe the king's condition. He insisted on seeing the queen, when, according to Lady Harcourt, the queen asked him what he meant by saying that the king was disturbed. He answered that he had cried a good deal. "If you call that being disturbed," said the queen, with readiness, "then this whole house is disturbed." Lady Harcourt describes the scene. "She received him with a courage and dignity that charmed me. Intimidated, hesitating and embarrassed, yet firm to the plan he has always pursued, he insisted that while any insanity remained he could not see that there was any material improvement. He said, too, that he formed his opinion partly from what he had heard, partly from what he had seen. She was then assured that the king kept talking in Latin, construing sentences, &c., on which the queen said she could not see what derangement there was in *that*. He protested he was sure her Majesty would like him to speak the truth. The queen declared her own strong love of truth alone made her agree to the bad accounts being published, and that the same motive now made her anxious that the world should share the comfort she felt in the king's recovery.

"Then followed a scene between Willis and Warren on the same point of dispute. Dr. Warren declared that he had given his opinion and would not depart from it. Willis said it was against common sense. Warren said, 'Then you say I have not common sense.' 'Upon this point,' replied the other, 'you have not shown it.' Warren called on the ladies to witness what had been said to him, and they could only express their concern at the unpleasant situation of things. The queen has told me she never will see him again. To do him justice, he was respectful in his manner to her, and constrained the rage which evidently shook his frame when I saw him again below stairs." How inflamed the passions were, and how difficult it was to act impartially, may be gathered from the feeling and impressions of that amiable and moderate man, Sir Gilbert Elliot, later Lord Minto. He seems to have been thoroughly permeated with all the prejudices of his party. We will contrast his account of this curious incident, which is made to assume a different complexion.

"Warren," he says, "when he went to Kew, was desired by Willis to sign a report which was ready written, that the king was better. He refused, saying it was not his opinion—that he seemed better in his health, but as to his disorder there was no change, and he was surprised at their preparing a report for him before consulting him. Willis told him that it was the queen who had

ordered that it should be signed. Warren persisted in
his refusal, and Willis still urged the queen's authority,
with threats as from her, that it would be worse for him
if he did not comply. Warren then desired to see the
queen, whom he found white with rage, and she asked
him in an angry voice what he meant by refusing to
sign. He gave the same reason as before, that his health
was better, but his mind not improved. The queen
said that others thought differently, and asked for his
reasons. The physician mentioned the king's conversation had been incoherent, and in other respects showed
insanity. The queen insisted on knowing exactly what
it was. Warren replied that it was impossible that he
could repeat it. She said she supposed it was something
improper, and again requested to be told, but the physician still refused, and at last was allowed to go. He was
followed out, however, by two old ladies, Lady Charlotte
Finch and Lady Harcourt, who told him they were sent
by the queen to learn what was this conversation. He
told them that Hawkins, the king's surgeon, had heard
much more of it, and referred them to him. Hawkins
was accordingly sent for, and being asked the same questions, made the same coy resistance, assuring them that
he could not bring his mouth to pronounce such things
in the presence of ladies."

All which was, of course, Warren's own story told to
the prince and the prince's friends. To other incidents
picked up by him in his visits were given the same
jaundiced complexion.

In December, 1788, Sir Gilbert wrote : " Willis has done all sorts of real mountebank things. On Saturdays he had the Princess Emily, of nine years old, brought to the king. As soon as she was within his reach he caught her up in his arms and swore that no power on earth should ever separate them again. The girl was terrified, and so were the bystanders, and they could not get the child away till they had promised to bring the queen. She was brought, and the king behaved exactly in the same way, catching hold of her and swearing that nothing should ever part them. The queen fell into fits, and they were obliged to separate them by main force, and the king was for the first time put into a strait-waistcoat, and continued raving for a consider- able time. When he saw Warren he made a remark- able speech, saying that he had put it on himself ; that a man who put it on could never wear the crown again." We may be sure that Warren told this acceptable story. He repeated it to the prince, and to Jack Payne, who told it to the amiable but very partisan Elliot.

The body-guard of ladies round the queen were now held out as being engaged in a sort of conspiracy to prevent the truth being known. " Mrs. Harcourt," said Sir Gilbert, " was amusing herself all this time by going into fits, and by passing days in tears about the king. I allow," he adds, " all the natural compassion for the distress of the royal family, but it is pushed to a rage and fury completely nonsensical against poor us." And again : " Willis has been detected writing letters to ——,

QUEEN CHARLOTTE

(From the Picture by Sir W. Beechey, R.A.)

who has read them at White's to the M.P.'s, giving
assurance of the king's great amendment and of his
immediate recovery — and this in days when he
was in a strait-waistcoat. Warren has remonstrated."

From the attacking the ladies of the court it was
an easy stage to proceed to attacking the queen herself,
and the poor lady was presently assailed as being engaged
in an ignoble plot for concealing the king's serious
state, so as to secure the continuance of his powers in
her own hands. Everything she did was distrusted,
and everything Warren could pick up on his visits was
ingenuously coloured so as to support the views of the
faction. "She is playing a game," wrote Elliot, "and
has been all this time at the bottom of the cabals and
intrigues against the prince. It is believed that she is ready
to accept the regency. One principal engine of the in-
triguers is the opinion which they contrive to maintain
in the public, that the king's recovery is to be expected
with certainty," and it cannot be denied that there was
much indiscretion and passion in the proceedings of the
court party. But what seems amazing was the open,
unblushing way in which the queen was denounced at
Brookes' and other resorts, as being at the bottom of all
the mischief. Sir Gilbert Elliot wrote in perfect good
faith : "Dr. Willis was brought about him for the purpose, the other physicians not being sufficiently subser-
vient, and he being a noted shot with the long-bow, and
besides being a quack. You see by this news the queen

is set at the head of a strong separate party or faction
against the government of the country."

And here was yet another anxiety for the queen in
her perilous task, the failing spirit and strength of the
aged Dr. Willis, the king's faithful friend and shield.
He was beginning to sink and lose heart, the attack
was so persistent and unrelenting; he was old and weary,
and was talking of withdrawing altogether.   This was a
real anxiety for the family, as without his trusty support
they would have been altogether unprotected.

But not only Sir Gilbert, but Burke himself
nourished these suspicions of the queen's artifices.
When the bill for committing the care of the king and
of the household to the queen was passed, he thundered
again and again against the opportunities it gave her
for deception. Not content with this insinuation, he
concluded with saying, " I don't suspect her of ever
intentionally acting with impropriety, but situations and
temptations may pervert the purest mind and draw it
aside from the path of rectitude.   Led on, step by step,
to commit these acts, like Macbeth after the murder,—

> " ' I am in blood
> Steept so far, that I should wade no more ;
> Returning were as tedious as go o'er—'

so *they* found themselves inclined to proceed, from a
want of courage to retrace their steps."

Again let us hear Sir Gilbert on the Regency Bill.   " It
surpassed," he said, " all that we conceived possible even
from Pitt.   Nobody but the queen will have the power

of *seeing* the king at all, except those she puts about him, and she will dismiss all the physicians except Dr. Willis, and perhaps one other to attend now and then, whom she thinks she can depend on. Even her own council are not to have a right to see the king, but are to take the accounts from the physicians.—that is to say, from Dr. Willis. When the queen chooses to declare that the king has recovered, the king may summon a certain number of Privy Councillors, to be selected and named by himself—that is, by the queen and Dr. Willis—and he may then declare his intention to resume the government; after which a proclamation is to be issued, and the regency is to be at an end at once. The scheme is calculated to enable the queen and Mr. Pitt to reinstate the king whether he will or not. They will then get him to nominate a regency, and probably to appoint the queen regent."

That partisan spirit should have so blinded this amiable and sensible man to imagine such a nonsensical plan as this, seems almost incredible. For it is plain that the queen could never have been able to carry out successfully such a plot as this ; indeed such notions could never have entered her head.

A few days later Sir Gilbert is angry because the queen was made guardian of the younger part of the royal family; "and they have given her all the houses and gardens in the country, *which gives her the patronage* of the rangers, housekeepers, apartments, &c."

Through all this long struggle, the king, it is plain,

was gradually being restored to his reason. The bulletins became more and more favourable. The Regency Bill, however, went on, but the court party began to feel quite secure as to the result. Naturally, the princes, as their hopes seemed so likely to be baffled, grew more distrustful. They wished to see with their own eyes, under pretence of a filial visit, the state of their father; but they were refused admission, on the ground of the agitation it would produce, and also because the king's occasionally rambling speeches would be distorted.

It is almost amusing to see how they were baffled in these schemes, and how faithfully the queen's ladies stood by their mistress. Failing the king, they determined to see the queen, and on January 28th, 1789, were admitted. Lady Harcourt describes the meeting :—.

"We had some great visitors yesterday," she writes ; "I got the doctor (Willis) clear off. They sent no page to announce their arrival. I fancy they hoped to see the queen alone. The *abord* on each side was *à la glace.*" She had to keep the conversation going by talking of Mrs. Siddons, Mrs. Abingdon, otherwise there would have been a most painful silence. When it came to four they announced that " it was dinner time," and took their leave. In the library they found Mr. Harcourt, and told him that the king was not at all better. Mr. Harcourt assured them that he was. "Aye," they answered, " *so old Willis says.*" "Not only Dr. Willis," was the reply, " but Sir L. Pepys told me the same thing this morning."

When the Regency Bill was passed, or sufficiently advanced, there was a trying scene in store for the harassed queen. It had been settled that she was to have control of the king, direction of his household, with a very handsome provision, and was to be assisted by a sort of council of notables or advisers. A deputation of the Lords and Commons waited on her to announce these arrangements. " She was agitated," her lady-in-waiting tells us, " but endeavoured to command herself, and went through the scene as well as one could expect. In her reply, which was conventional, she spoke of the momentous trust reposed in her, and said it would be a great consolation to her to receive the aid of a council."

The princes were at last admitted to see their father, but not for six weeks. Of this visit to the king the prince's friends gave a version of their own. " They had gone down constantly to Kew, but were always refused on one pretext or another, though the Chancellor and many other strangers they said were let in. The prince at last wrote to the queen, and after many shifts and delays, the prince and the Duke of York were yesterday (February 22nd, 1789) admitted. The meeting was extremely affecting and affectionate on both sides." The king had to wait at the door before he could collect himself to enter, embraced both and shed tears on their faces. " Both the princes were much touched by the scene." He avoided business, talked of horses, soldiers, &c. " The queen was present, and walking to and fro in the room with a countenance and manner of great dissatisfaction; and the king every now and then went to her in a submissive way and spoke in a soothing sort of tone, for she has acquired the same sort of drilling over him that Willis and his men have— and the king's mind is totally subdued and in a state of the greatest weakness and subjection. It is given out even by the prince's friends that they observed nothing *wrong* or irrational in this visit, and it is material that they should not be thought to publish the contrary. It is not entirely true, however, as the king made several slips, one of which was that he told them he was the Chancellor. This circumstance is not to be mentioned for the reasons just given." Thus Sir G. Elliot.

These distressing conflicts show how the most trifling matter could be twisted into accusations. On one morning when the physicians had gathered for consultation and their usual wrangle, the party was at breakfast, and were detained some time finishing this meal after the queen had sent for them. It was given out that the queen was very angry at the delay, though it was proved that she really thought they had finished breakfast. Warren said to Mrs. Harcourt " that he was afraid he had offended her Majesty." She, thinking he was referring to the breakfast delay, said, " Oh no, the queen is very well satisfied." On which Warren artfully reported in town that the queen was now sorry for her behaviour and had apologized to him! This may have occurred, and no doubt there was some such purpose in the mind of the prince's set ; but it will be understood how easily party passion would exaggerate some trifling incident of the kind. It must be admitted there were proceedings of the queen and her following which were indiscreet and betrayed the fanatic passion which influenced the party. It should have been remembered on both sides that the struggle had taken the unseemly shape of a contest between mother and son, which, if unavoidable, ought to have been regulated by the greatest tact and decorum. When the royal party moved from Windsor to Kew, the prince very properly collected all his father's papers and jewels and sealed them up in a place of security. This proceeding was made the ground of an accusation that he had secured and appropriated the king's property.[1]

It is characteristic of the royal pair that even at this crisis they should have kept in mind their old serious pursuits and tastes. Thomas Willis was a clergyman, and gave his patient a sermon of his own to read, which both king and queen were so interested in, that they must send it at once to their friend Dr. Hurd. How unaffected is the queen's letter :—

"Feb. 7th, 1789.—When I was last night with the king, he inquired very anxiously after you, and seemed pleased to hear of your having been at Kew, to inform yourself after him. He also gave me the sermon for you of Mr Thomas Willis, and ordered me to send it as soon as possible, and to express how much he wished to know your

---

[1] The list of articles, which consisted of a few jewelled orders, is now in the British Museum.

opinion about it.   I am likewise to introduce this new
acquaintance of ours to you, and I hope, nay, I am pretty
sure that you will like him, as he really is a very modest
man, and by his conduct in this house gains everybody's approbation.   My good sir, this letter was wrote
yesterday, but no opportunity was found to send it ; the
consequence of which is that the sermon is brought by
its author, whom I hope you will approve of meeting."

After this meeting between the king and his sons had
been happily got over, the two princes continued their
attempts to have further access.   Early in March the
Duke of York saw him again, and reported to all that
the king's conversation was made up of childish remarks
—such as, that he intended setting out for Hanover ;
that "he had given orders for the cabriolet for the
queen *to drive herself.*"   Some time before the prince had
given the queen some papers which he had drawn up
for his own vindication, and which, he pressed, should be
laid before the king.   In the face of these worrying
importunities, which were difficult to resist, the queen
made a gallant stand.   She knew—as her sons knew
very well—that details of business were as yet highly
dangerous for one in the king's state; nor did the young
men note how inconsistent with the stories they were
circulating of the king's "childishness" was the suppo-
sition that he could understand the papers they were
forcing on him.

The Prince of Wales, however, continued to insist,
pressing for an interview.   "The queen," his partisans

repeated, " had sent some shabby excuse for not answering that day." She was, no doubt, waiting to consult the Chancellor. She said that she had mentioned the matter of the papers to the king, but he had not asked for them ; but that should he do so, she would lay them before him. She passed by his request for an interview. On the same evening, however, came a letter from her Majesty, enclosing one from the king to her, " written with his own hand, but evidently dictated by Pitt, or some of his people."

Thus Sir Gilbert, who with the rest of the faction seems to have learnt of every step in the matter in a few hours after it occurred. The king in this letter referred to all the trouble he had given her, and that he would strive not to give her any further anxieties. He therefore was not " inclined to enter on any business that might agitate him." These family letters were shown about at the club, and were pronounced " clumsy artifices." It was a transparent " put off." Why should the king, being in the same house with her, write to the queen? The resolution not to admit the princes seemed sensible enough, and were it only to prevent a relapse, which it almost seemed as though the opposing faction were eager to bring about, it was natural at least that such should be the opinion of the queen and *her* faction.

It must have been inexpressibly welcome to this faithful lady to find the king every day improving in health through her wakeful guard. The whole city was now illuminated and given up to rejoicings ; the ambassadors

came to present congratulations, and the king bore these
tests very well.   The baffled princes, who had to look on
and ruefully join in the rejoicings, presently lost all
restraint.   The prince " had a smart little tussle with
his mother, in which they came to strong and open
declarations of hostility.   He told her that she had
connected herself with his enemies, and had entered into
plans for destroying and disgracing him and all her
children ; that she countenanced misrepresentations of his
conduct to the king, and prevented the explanations he
wished to give.   She was violent and lost her temper,
and her conversation ended, I believe, by her saying that
she would not be the channel of anything that either he
or the Duke of York had to say, &c."   However we may
deplore these painful recriminations, we must have
indulgence for the wife and mother, who felt that her
hour of triumph had come, and was not inclined to spare
her unfilial child.   Even his henchman, Sir Gilbert,
thought the prince's behaviour indecorous.

It must have been a fresh element in her triumph to
see at all the festivals the ladies of the opposition almost
compelled to sport in their caps the motto, " God save
the King," and also to have to go to court and ruefully
congratulate.

CHAPTER X.

THE DUKE OF YORK'S DUEL.

BUT now, at the end of March, arose a more serious question. There was to be a grand concert at Windsor, to which the " opposition " princes were not at once invited, when the Duke of York, as usual in search of a grievance, once more sought the queen to make his complaints. She gave him a message from his Majesty to the effect, that she was to inform them there was to be a concert, to which they were welcome, if they liked to come, but it was right to let them know that it was intended for those " *who had supported us* through the late business, and therefore you may not wish to come." This cold form of invitation was written down by the duke to be shown about. The duke turned it off, saying that it applied to the whole nation, as they had all supported the king according to their respective ideas of support. " No! no !" said her Majesty, " I don't choose to be misunderstood—I mean those who have voted for us and no one else."

Another edifying scene followed. Her son got very

angry, defended himself and his brother, and finally said that he would not go, but the prince might if he liked.

Now here again there was nothing that was altogether unreasonable. The concert was intended as a loyal " demonstration," a celebration of victory, and this the queen felt that it was only fair to give her sons notice of. They would naturally feel an awkwardness in such a situation and in such company. But the answer was unfairly " twisted " and made capital of.

There was much council-holding on the news, the Prince of Wales and his brother being " both in a violent rage on this attack of the queen, which charged them in plain words with being enemies to the king." And they at first thought of showering fresh papers of complaint on the king—" strong measures," as they termed it, were to be taken. But Burke and the cooler heads intervened—it was thought unwise to come to an open rupture, which would give excuse for excluding them altogether.

It was astonishing, however, what animosity prevailed, for it was learned, or said to be learned from Colonel Goldsworthy, that the king had said that the princes were invited, and should always consider themselves as invited to everything, as of course, but had said nothing of classes of persons or of those who had supported them. " So that this," wrote Sir G. Elliot, " was an addition of the queen's, intended, I suppose, to prevent them accepting. You see the princes are represented in the king's family by the queen herself as enemies of their father, who is watched like a prisoner, and is never out of sight of one or other of the head keepers, i.e. the queen." The Duke of York at last sent a conciliatory letter, saying that he would be glad to go, and so the matter passed over.

Meanwhile, at all the rejoicings, balls at White's, galas, thanksgiving at St. Paul's, and other exciting scenes, the king appeared and acquitted himself fairly well.

But in May there arose out of these cabals yet another scandal, which became the talk of the town. This was the well-known duel of the Duke of York with Colonel Lennox, an extraordinary, unprecedented business.

Colonel Lennox, afterwards Duke of Richmond, was an ardent partisan of the court, and showed his feeling in the most thorough fashion. He was heard at clubs and other places openly attacking the princes for their behaviour, sometimes even in their presence. He behaved throughout this exciting business with the resolution of an old hand, but he was only a young officer not more than five-and-twenty, the son of Lord George Lennox.[1]

This contention of kings' men and princes' men rather suggests the state of things described in Dumas' historical romances, where Cardinal Richelieu had his followers who were constantly fighting the opposite faction. According to Sir G. Elliot, Lennox had been insulting the princes "in the most scurrilous and blackguard way"—an absurd exaggeration. "You

---

[1] He was married this year to a lady of the house of Gordon, on which alliance the present Duke of Richmond founded his claim to the revival of the Dukedom of Gordon.

must know," he adds, "that this is the tone of the court, or queen's party," who thought they would have no better way of recommending themselves to favour. It seems that Mr. Lennox was "forced into the Coldstream Guards"—that is, was transferred to that regiment by the king's order, the forcing being that the Duke of York, who was colonel, had not been consulted.

It was of course understood that it was war to the knife between the houses, and that the duke was not to expect any favour or consideration—that the time was come for his Majesty to reward his adherents. The duke made remonstrances which were not attended to. However, when the matter was finally settled, the duke received the officer in a friendly way, saying handsomely that though he had opposed the entrance of the new officer as a matter of principle, he was glad to have him under his command. The *frondeur* Lennox, however, answered him that it was the king's pleasure he was there, and that was enough for him—a speech that shows what was the feeling abroad.

St. Leger, at their club, at last said to him bluntly, "Why don't you say this to some of us who can answer you?" of which speech Colonel Lennox took no notice. This incident was repeated to the duke, who went about saying that "Colonel Lennox had submitted to language that no gentleman would put up with."

In this fashion the matter became inflamed into a regular quarrel. The duke's remark was reported to the colonel, who was certainly a man of high daring spirit, and not at all likely to accept "language that no gentleman would put up with." He walked up to his colonel on parade and before the other officers brought him to an account for these words, and insisted on an explanation, but the duke merely ordered him to his place. Later, in the barrack room, Lennox again renewed the matter, demanding what were the words the duke alluded to and who was the person who spoke them.

The duke declined to help him in any way, saying he must very well know these things himself. Lennox then complained of the great hardship of his position— for the duke was the king's son, and therefore protected, whereas in the case of a private person he could have satisfaction. The duke begged that that should be no objection, and hoped he would consider him as a private gentleman. This the other said he could not do.

Lennox next wrote to all the persons who had been present, asking for their recollection of the matter. This proved unsatisfactory and led to nothing, on which he took the extraordinary step of sending Lord Winchelsea with a formal challenge to the duke. The king used to thank God that none of his children lacked courage save one—whom it was not difficult to name. But the duke showed no lack of this quality, and cheerfully consented to "give him satisfaction." A meeting was arranged. The colonel's pistol ball actually passed through the duke's curl. So he had a very narrow escape indeed. The duke fired in the air. On this it was oddly suggested that the duke should admit that Colonel Lennox had behaved

" like a man of honour," but the duke declined to go out of his record, declaring that he had come there to give him the satisfaction he asked for, and that if he desired another shot he was welcome to it.   The other said that he could not fire at the duke if the latter did not return his fire.   On which they parted.   Such was this extraordinary business, which went within a hair's breadth almost of having a fatal issue.   We can imagine what a tumult there would have been had the king's son been shot by a subject.   The faction rather unfairly distorted the fact that a travelling carriage and four laden with imperials, &c., was waiting to carry away the colonel in case his shot had taken effect.   It was insisted that this was proof of his deliberate purpose, but it was merely a prudent provision for his own safety, as he would have been in great peril.   The Prince of Wales, after he had heard the account from his brother, set off for Kew with this choice " tit-bit " of news.   He sent in a message that he wished to speak with the king alone, just for five minutes.   " Very well," said the poor worried king, " but I must go up to the queen first."   This speech seems to have struck the faction with disgust, for here was evidence of tyranny ; but he felt that he really needed her advice and supervision at every step.   To let the king see his son alone, who might scare or alarm him, and who, in fact, came charged with a startling piece of news, was not to be thought of.   So the royal visitor found himself introduced to the whole party, princesses and all, drawn up to receive him.

The prince proceeded to recount all that had occurred, and even injudiciously described how the ball had passed through the curl, which caused the king to shudder, and he even gave a short cry of terror. But according to her son's report, the queen, who was at the window, looking out, "heard it all with perfect composure, and when he had finished said that *she* understood that it was all the duke's *own fault*, and that according to her account of the matter he had shown more eagerness to fight Mr. Lennox than Mr. Lennox to fight him." This was held out as very being callous, but it was plain she had heard the story before, and she moreover felt it necessary to tone down, for the sake of the king, the melodramatic story which the prince had been rehearsing. He retorted that his brother was not likely to have provoked the conflict, as in that case he would not have fired in the air. But he brought back to town a report of the interview to the effect that neither king nor queen had exhibited the slightest feeling of satisfaction at their son's deliverance, and this account was rather indecently retailed to all the friends and supporters. Of course the poor queen had been on her guard, and knew well that whatever she did or said would be distorted and set down to the worst motives. According to the Prince of Wales' statement, he himself had warned the queen a week before that some mischief might ensue—with a view, said his followers, that it might be stopped by authority. This was likely enough, as the matter was of common notoriety. But how was the queen to stop

such a business, and to tell the king would only agitate
him ?

Nothing is more extraordinary in this internecine
conflict than the fashion in which it destroyed all the
natural family feeling, even in the breast of the excellent
queen.   Here was a duel in which her own son's life
was in peril ; he had the narrowest escape ; yet she
looked on coldly, and showed no sign of satisfaction—
or at least disguised it successfully—when he came out
of it unscathed.   She no doubt considered he was one of
the band that had virtually been compassing his father's
destruction.

A remarkable incident too, in this view, was that the
duke's second, Lord Winchelsea, was actually one of her
own household, and seems to have incurred no dis-
approval for what he had done.

It was agreed that the duke had behaved with due
courage, according to duelling canons.   When he found
his brother anxiously awaiting the issue, he excused
himself from giving a full account, saying that he had to
go off and play tennis.

The meeting between the queen and her eldest son was
of a very painful kind.   She could not make up her
mind to see him—she dreaded the agitation, especially as
he insisted on an audience with the greatest excitement
and vehemence.   She gave way at last, and in answer to
his complaints, summoned Miss Goldsworthy and her
equerries to answer any questions he chose to put.   He
did not kiss her hand, as was usual, but hammered with

his stick on the floor and loudly condemned everything
that had been done.

In a day or two the Duke of York came himself, and
was received alone by the king with the greatest marks
of affection and tenderness.   " When the queen came in,
she made no remark on the transaction, good or bad."
It was said indeed that she made a light remark as to
" whether Boodles' ball last night was crowded."   All
which is consistent with her character as a cold, resolved
person, and who could not forget that the transaction
was one intended to damage her cause.

The court ball was to begin at eight o'clock, but
at seven arrived the Prince of Wales in a great fume,
who insisted on seeing the queen at once, though he was
told she was dressing ; she, however, admitted him.   He
came to ask her, or rather to require her, not to receive
Colonel Lennox to the ball, on account of the duel !   The
queen, however, was not to be moved, and said that she
could not interfere in the matter until the king was
apprised of his business.   When Mr. Pitt arrived, she
sent him to the king, who decided that matters should
go on as before.   The prince returned to town quite
exasperated.

All these trials had their effect : her hair had
turned grey ; she was depressed to a degree, and could
hardly be induced to go out in a carriage.   More extraordinary, according to the same authorities, was the
queen's marked partiality for the other combatant.   At
the French ambassador's she not only received him very

graciously, " but afterwards, when there was no occasion for it, kissed her fan to him two or three times, half the length of the room, taking pains to make her favour as conspicuous as she could." [1]

But what was all this to the scene at the St. James's ball! All the party, " royals " and others, were figuring in the country dance, the Prince of Wales with his sister, Princess Royal, " going down the middle " and " turning " everybody according to the form. Of a sudden the royal heir came to Colonel Lennox and his partner, when the prince stopped, and the princess being about to be " turned " by the colonel, her partner abruptly drew her away and passed to the bottom. The Duke of Clarence did the same, but the Duke of York danced on. After this exhibition, the prince went up to the queen, having, however, apologized to Colonel Lennox's partner. Her Majesty asked, we may presume as an explanation of his behaviour, was he tired? He said, " Not at all." She supposed, then, he found it too hot. He said that in such company it was impossible not to find it too hot. After this display of petulance, the queen said, " I suppose you would wish me to break up the ball?" " The best thing you can do, madam," was his reply. And so the ball was brought to an abrupt conclusion.

In all these painful and unbecoming transactions it can only be said that there was on both sides a sad lack of discretion, and even decency. If it be against all the *bienséances* that family linen should not be washed in

[1] " Elliot's Life and Letters," i. 320.

public, it is still more incumbent that those in charge of the royal linen should abstain from doing so. The queen, much tried as she had been, was certainly carried away by the mad passions of the hour, and, whatever were her feelings as to the unfilial behaviour of her sons, might have been discreet enough at least to conceal them. It should be considered, however, that these stories came from her enemies, who were watching and exaggerating everything she did, and whose prejudices made them see every action of hers in the worst light.

The queen naturally doing her best to make friends for the king, was credited with making exertions to form a party and strengthen her faction. Sir Gilbert Elliot, an amiable man, but prejudiced in everything that concerned her, gives rather an amusing account of these efforts ; though, it will be seen, there is not much harm in the matter. All her friends, he said, were canvassing like agents and candidates before an election. There was a certain important Mrs. Legge who had been absent for many years, and " the queen had got people to tell her that her absence had not effaced the impression which the pleasure of her company at court had given her ; and that one of the things she thought of with pleasure was the prospect which Mrs. Legge's recovery gave of enjoying this satisfaction again. Meanwhile Mrs. Harcourt, and the Digbys and others all ply her with courtship and flatteries. The queen's speech nearly vanquished her with a blow, and she has twice put

herself in the queen's way with a *bandeau* of ' God save
the King ' in her cap."

One evening Mr. Windham and Sir Gilbert called on
this lady, and while talking with her were interrupted
by news that Mrs. Harcourt was below, and desired to
see her only for a single minute.   " There was an evident
confusion in our party : Mrs. Legge seemed distressed
what to do with us, and not to like being caught with
such rebels in such *privacy*. Windham and I were
accordingly shoved into another room, like lovers in a
play when the husband comes home unexpectedly.
When Mrs. Harcourt retired, Mrs. Legge came creeping
in and released us. I found Mrs. Harcourt's business
was to settle Mrs. Legge's visit to St. Leonards at some
time when there should be nobody else and they should
have her all to themselves."

After this sad and trying episode, it was natural that
touring and change of scene should be prescribed for the
afflicted king.   A long and extended tour followed, during
which the king was attended by nearly all his family,
and in a very simple and unaffected way mixed with his
subjects, visited many places, and enjoyed himself
thoroughly.

The little watering-place of Weymouth was selected as
his place of residence, the Duke of Gloucester having a
lodge there, which he lent to the king.   The royal party
started at seven in the morning of June 25th, and
reached Lyndhurst about three.   With the king and
queen travelled the three elder princesses and a large

suite, Lord and Lady Courtown, the Ladies Waldegrave,
Colonels Goldsworthy and Gwyn. At Lyndhurst they
were received by the whole population, and according to
an ancient custom two milk-white greyhounds with
gold collars were presented to the king. Here they dined
in full view of the crowd, the windows being thrown wide
open, and afterwards walked through the village to
exhibit themselves to the rustics. Next Southampton
and Lymington were visited, also Salisbury, and finally
Weymouth was reached, where a splendid reception
awaited them. The king was delighted with the place
and the sea, and the beautiful view, and indeed was
always afterwards very partial to Weymouth.

CHAPTER XI.

ROYAL TOURS. ROYAL TASTES.

IN this year the royal family found special gratification in the very suitable marriage of their second son, the Duke of York, who had secured the hand of the sister of the reigning King of Prussia, Princess Frederica Charlotte. It had been better had this sensible lady fallen to the lot of his elder brother, and the country would at least have been spared thirty years' scandals.

At Weymouth the king bathed regularly, to the admiration of the town, a smack following his movements with a band on board, a compliment that must have amused the queen.

Mrs. Harcourt gives a sketch of the life at Weymouth. " The king's bathing agreed beyond anything with him. The princess also looks well, but the queen looks, I think, very ill, and by all accounts has been so low and languid that nothing but real illness can account for it. She always appears to me to look worse and worse every time I have seen her for the last half-year. Her foot is bad, but she walks a little. They have no society at all but those you know of. Mr. Pitt and Lord Grenville are here, but never asked in. The party has always been

the queen, princess royal, Lady Chesterfield and General
Harcourt at casino ; Princess Elizabeth, Lady Mary,
Lady Caroline, Colonel Gwyn at cribbage ; the king,
Colonel Garth, and Lord Chesterfield at piquet. Lord
and Lady Courtown and Princess Augusta have hitherto
played at piquet, but now I make a fourth. On Sunday,
at eight, we all went to the rooms, which is, without
exception, the oddest ceremony I ever saw. A very
large room, two or three hundred people, none of which,
except the two Lady Beauclerks and three or four men,
one ever heard of. It is a circle like a drawing-room
exactly, and there they stand or walk if they can for
about half an hour ; then go into the card room, which
opens into it, and where there are two or three tables.
The king and queen or princesses play, the people all
walking by the door and looking in, but not coming in.
The king walked about a little more ; and they all went
away at ten."

There is a pleasing picture of the royal family enjoying
themselves at the little country theatre of Weymouth,
whose interior suggests that of the Theatre Royal, Portsmouth, as depicted in "Nickleby." The Duke of York
had come down to see his parents, attended by Mr. Bunbury. Mrs. Jordan was to perform : Mr. Bunbury was
eager to see her, and the duke "imbibed his wishes" and
persuaded the royal family to go. An order was hastily
sent to the manager to get ready the royal box. On the
night the little house presented a brave show. The centre
boxes were filled by the royal party—their Majesties, the

duke and three princesses in the front rows, Lord Harcourt and Colonel "Fairly," Lord and Lady Courtown,
Lady Pembroke, and others of the retinue standing
behind—it was the etiquette that these poor people
should stand when on duty. The galleries were over
their heads, so that the honest folk above could not have
a glimpse of the royal party. But nothing could exceed
the general delight and enthusiasm—there were shouts
and hurrahs through the night. When we think that
these country theatres were either " boxes " of the Bijou
Theatre kind—something like the old theatre at Richmond—the whole must have the air of a family party,
and the king and queen were literally seated among their
subjects.

At this time another junketing was made—a visit to
Worcester, to Bishop Hurd, who was such a favourite of
the royal family. They were quartered at the palace, an
old house and not very large, so that the retinue had to be
lodged in the town, and the bishop himself and his family
had to find quarters elsewhere. The Festival was going
on, and the royal visitors—always ardent where music
was concerned—attended the oratorios and the evening
concerts. One night Quick, a favourite, would perform
at the little theatre ; next night there was Mrs. Wells. On
the 29th appeared Mrs. Siddons, in comedy characters—
an odd choice—but the queen did not care for high-
strung tragedies ; nor was this surprising. There is one
very pleasing picture of these enjoyments, and which
leaves a good impression of the good-hearted and simple

ways of their Majesties.   They had planned an expedition to Mr. Weld's seat, Lulworth Castle, to which
they went by sea.   Mrs. Siddons was to play Lady
Townley, and their party engaged to return for the performance.   The wind was not favourable, and, just as the
curtain was about to rise, the manager was aghast at
receiving a message that they had only reached Lulworth
at five o'clock.   They would try to be back in time, but
he was to begin with the farce.   The house was
crowded, but the audience waited most patiently.   The
farce was played : but no king.   It came to ten o'clock,
but both manager and audience determined to wait, and
did.   They at last were put ashore close by the theatre,
turned into Lady Pembroke's lodgings, where the king
sent for his wig and the queen for her maid, and finally
entered the theatre to a hurricane of applause, when the
play at last began.   This, it may be repeated, is an
interesting and even charming picture.

  Lady Harcourt, describing one of these nights, explains
the difficulties of this crowded state of things : one of
which was to provide that no persons should be in contact with the royal party.   This was arranged by filling
the boxes next the royal ones with friends or distinguished
persons of the neighbourhood.

  "To-day all go to the play.   I am to take the box on
one side of the queen, because they have not one
acquaintance here, and she might have a perfect stranger
(beside her), and Lady Courtown, instead of attending
her, is obliged to take the other side to sit next the king ;

for the same reason I am ordered to get acquainted with some Yorkshire people that are here (the great Tatton Egertons, with £30,000 a year), in order to get them to help this sitting business."

A spy, it was thought, had been sent down, who turned out to be a servant of the Duke of Devonshire. "He walked so close that some of the royal dependents got into talk with him, when he let out 'that he was sure the king was as bad as ever, only well guarded, and he would listen.' But when found out, he went away in great haste to disappoint the wicked wishes of his employers."

The queen had now to come back to her round of duties, with such spirit as she could bring to them, or with as little anticipation of evil as she could shut out. Fanny Burney is still the heroine of the court, and its most vivacious chronicler, and on her we must rely for the most spirited accounts of all that went forward. Her own intimate relations with the queen during this time constitute her the best of all the contemporary reporters. Though her accounts refer mainly to her own personal concerns, they present an excellent picture of her character and methods. Sometimes her Majesty would come and "look her up" at her rooms, entering without knocking—a privilege, it seems, of royalty. She would turn over her books, and criticize them. She always liked to hear Miss Burney talk of her literary friends. Next day she made her a present of Ogden's sermons, which Miss Burney said was a favourite with Dr. Johnson. "Oh, I am glad of that!" she exclaimed eagerly. But previously Miss Burney made a fresh mistake, for the worthy Bishop Hurd having arrived, whom she was expected to entertain at her table, she got rid of him and sent him to the equerries. She told the queen of this proceeding, " who made no comment."

Among the teachers at Windsor was a music-master named Webb, who gave the young princesses lessons in music. It is evidence of the kind charity of the king and queen that they employed this unhappy being, who was disfigured by an enormous nose, which spread half over his face. The queen herself used to tell how anxious she was that the princesses should not laugh at the afflicted musician. " When first Mr. Webb was to come to Sophia, I told her he had had some accident to disfigure his whole face, but I desired her to remember this was a misfortune for which he ought to be pitied, and she must be sure not to laugh at him, or stare at him. And she minded this very well, and behaved always very properly. But when Lady Cremorne was at the Lodge and Mr. Webb was announced, Sophia coloured very red, and ran up to Lady Cremorne and said to her in a whisper, ' Lady Cremorne, Mr. Webb has got a very great nose, but that is only to be pitied—so mind you don't laugh.' " The little princess was only nine years old.

One of the most pleasing characteristics of the king and queen was their eager curiosity and longing even to know and patronize such of their subjects who were distinguished for worth and learning. Persons like

Mrs. Hannah More or Mrs. Trimmer, Doctors Johnson
and Beattie, and Miss Burney, found the most cordial
appreciation.   In their absence, they were talked about
and inquired after ; and all details as to their character
and pursuits were gathered up with interest, an interest
that was based on a thorough acquaintance with their
writings and acts.   Any one who was on the side of
morals and loyalty was sure of being encouraged.   To
some persons their Majesties " took a fancy," as it is
called ; but this was by no means of a transitory kind.
It is a surprise that the famous interview with Dr. Johnson
at the library at Buckingham House did not lead to further
and closer intimacy : the reason probably was that the
sturdy doctor was too independent in his ways, and
scarcely supple enough in his approaches to royalty.
Dr. Beattie, who was more plastic, has left an account
of his interview, which is insipid enough, and in odd
contrast to the dramatic tone of the great doctor's.

He thus describes the meeting : " Tuesday, the 24th of
August, I set out for Dr. Majendie's at Kew Green.   The
doctor told me that he had not seen the king yesterday,
but had left a note in writing to intimate that I was at
his house to-day; and that one of the king's pages had
come to him this morning to say, ' that his Majesty
would see me a little after twelve.'

" At twelve, the doctor and I went to the king's house
at Kew.   We had been only a few minutes in the hall,
when the king and queen came in from an airing; and
as they passed through the hall, the king called to me

by name, and asked how long it was since I came from town. I answered about an hour. 'I shall see you,' says he, 'in a little.' The doctor and I waited a considerable time (for the king was busy), and then we were called into a large room, furnished as a library, where the king was walking about, and the queen sitting in a chair. We were received in the most gracious manner possible by both their Majesties. I had the honour of a conversation with them (nobody else being present but Dr. Majendie) for upwards of an hour, on a great variety of topics, in which both the king and queen joined, with a degree of cheerfulness, affability, and ease that was to me surprising, and soon dissipated the embarrassment which I felt at the beginning of the conference. They both complimented me, in the highest terms, on my essay, which, they said, was a book they always kept by them; and the king said he had one copy of it at Kew, and another in town, and immediately went and took it down from a shelf. I found it was the second edition. 'I never stole a book but one,' said his Majesty, 'and that was yours (speaking to me); I stole it from the queen, to give it to Lord Hertford to read.' He had heard that the sale of 'Hume's Essays' had failed since my book was published; and I told him what Mr. Strahan had told me in regard to that matter. He had even heard of my being in Edinburgh last summer, and how Mr. Hume was offended on the score of my book. He asked many questions about the second part of the 'Essay,' and when it would be ready for the

press.   I gave him, in a short speech, an account of the
plan of it; and said, my health was so precarious I could
not tell when it would be ready, as I had many books to
consult before I could finish it; but that, if my health
was good, I thought I might bring it to a conclusion in
two or three years.   He asked how long I had been in
composing my ' Essay,' praised the caution with which
it was written, and said he did not wonder that it had
employed me five or six years.   He asked about my
poems.   I said there was only one poem of my own on
which I set any value (meaning the ' Minstrel '), and that
it was first published about the same time with the
' Essay.'   My other poems, I said, were incorrect, being
but juvenile .pieces, and of little consequence, even in
my own opinion.   We had much conversation on moral
subjects, from which both their Majesties let it appear
that they were warm friends to Christianity; and so little
inclined to infidelity, that they could hardly believe that
any thinking man could really be an atheist, unless he
could bring himself to believe that he made himself—a
thought which pleased the king exceedingly, and he
repeated it several times to the queen.   He asked
whether anything had been written against me.   I
spoke of the late pamphlet, of which I gave an account,
telling him that I never had met with any man who
had read it, except one quaker.   This brought on some
discourse about the quakers, whose moderation and
mild behaviour the king and queen commended.   I
was asked many questions about the Scots universities,

the revenues of the Scots clergy, their mode of praying and preaching; the medical college of Edinburgh, Dr. Gregory (of whom I gave a particular character) and Dr. Cullen; the length of our vacation at Aberdeen, and the closeness of our attendance during the winter; the number of students that attend my lectures; my mode of lecturing, whether from notes or completely written lectures: about Mr. Hume, and Dr. Robertson, and Lord Kinnoul, and the Archbishop of York, &c. His Majesty asked me what I thought of my new acquaintance, Lord Dartmouth ?   I said there was something in his air and manner which I thought not only agreeable, but enchanting, and that he seemed to me to be one of the best of men—a sentiment in which both their Majesties heartily joined. ' They say that Lord Dartmouth is an enthusiast,' said the king; ' but surely he says nothing on the subject of religion, but what every Christian may, and ought to say.' He asked whether I did not think the English language on the decline at present ?   I answered in the affirmative, and the king agreed, and named the *Spectator* as one of the best standards in the language. When I told him that the Scots clergy sometimes prayed a quarter, or even half an hour at a time, he asked whether that did not lead them into repetitions?   I said it often did. ' That,' said he, ' I don't like in prayers; and excellent as our liturgy is, I think it somewhat faulty in that respect.' ' Your Majesty knows,' said I, ' that three services are joined in one in the ordinary church service, which is one cause of those repetitions.' 'True,' he replied, 'and that circumstance also makes the service too long.' From this, he took occasion to speak of the composition of the Church liturgy, on which he very justly bestowed the highest commendation. 'Observe,' his Majesty said, 'how flat those occasional prayers are, that are now composed, in comparison with the old ones.' When I mentioned the smallness of the Church livings in Scotland, he said, 'he wondered how men of liberal education would choose to become clergymen there,' and asked, 'whether in the remote parts of the country, the clergy in general were not very ignorant?' I answered, 'No, for that education was very cheap in Scotland, and that the clergy in general were men of good sense and competent learning.' He asked whether we had any good preachers at Aberdeen? I said yes, and named Campbell and Gerard, with whose names, however, I did not find that he was acquainted. Dr. Majendie mentioned Dr. Oswald's 'Appeal,' with commendation; I praised it too, and the queen took down the name, with a view to send for it. I was asked whether I knew Dr. Oswald? I answered, I did not, and said that my book was published before I read his; that Dr. Oswald was well known to Lord Kinnoul, who had often proposed to make us acquainted. We discussed a great many other topics; for the conversation, as before observed, lasted for upwards of an hour, without any intermission. The queen bore a large share in it."

Sending the doctor's book to a friend, the queen accompanied it with this sensible letter :—

" The book which accompanies this note is an essay
on the ' Immortality of the Soul,' which I received on
Saturday last.   It appears to be against Mr. Hume's,
Voltaire's and Rousseau's principles, and chiefly against
the first of these authors.   As I am not in the least
acquainted with the writings of those unhappy men, I
must beg the bishop to give me his opinion upon this
latter trait, as the author of it will not publish his name
until he knows the reception of it by some able and
understanding men.   I do also send the letter of the
author, who appears modest and well-meaning; and more
should be said about him, I believe, but the dedication
being to me, I might be suspected of being guided by
flattery: you know I hate bribery and corruption ; but
being corrupted by flattery is worse than money, as it is
an open avowal of a corrupted heart, and I hope you do
not suspect me of that.   I shall be glad to hear of your
being well after the fatigue of yesterday."

And again to her favourite bishop :—

" MY LORD,—I never wished so much to exercise my
power and commands as to-day, but I hope you will
believe me when I say that this desire does not arise
from any tyrannical inclination, but from a real regard
for you.   The wintry feel of this day makes me
desirous of preventing you exposing yourself to-morrow
morning at court, where I could only see, but not enjoy
your company, which pleasure I beg to have any other
day, when less inconvenient and less pernicious to your
health."

Another of these interesting interviews, where we are introduced to the king and queen, and hear them talking in the easiest and most unaffected fashion, was vouchsafed to Mr. Hardinge, a well-known lawyer of the time. He thus describes it :—

"I arrived at the queen's Lodge at twelve, and was carried to the equerry's room. Colonel Digby came to me, civil, and gentleman-like. He chatted with me for half an hour, and when he left me, said 'he would let the king know through General Harcourt that I was there.' In a few minutes I was gallanted upstairs into Madame Schwellenbergen's dining apartment. There I found General Harcourt, who is a very agreeable man. He told me, 'that when the king (who was going to the castle to receive the address of the clergy) should come out of his apartment, he would let him know, and receive his commands.'

"In a quarter of an hour two royal coaches came to the door ; and an equerry handed the queen into the first. The king followed her, without a thought, apparently, of poor me. Princess Royal and Princess Augusta followed. This filled the first coach. No. 2 had Princess Elizabeth and a bedchamber-woman. Then, a-foot, my friends Digby and Harcourt. When they were flown, the porter came to me, and said, 'General Harcourt had named me to the king ; but that his Majesty being in a great hurry, had said nothing. That, if I pleased, I might wait till his Majesty's return, which,' the porter said, 'would be in one hour and a

half.' This, I thought, was as much as to say, 'If you
go, you will not be missed.' In half an hour Mrs.
Schwellenbergen's German footman came to lay the
cloth, and produced the dining apparatus. For want of
occupation, I formed an acquaintance with him, and
learned that Madame Schwellenbergen sat at the head
of the table; the Misses Burney and Planta right and
left of her, and any visitor at bottom. The room is
pretty enough, and clean, but furnished with a cheap
kind of paper, and linen curtains. *Observing a large piece
of German bread, I fell to, and ate a pound of it.* The
hour and a half having expired, the regals returned; and
then I heard the queen most condescendingly say, 'Do
find out Mr. Hardinge, and beg of him to come and see
us.' Her butler, out of livery, came to me, and desired
me to follow him. I went through a very handsome
apartment into another most beautifully fitted up, with
a ceiling of the modern work, 'done,' as the king told
me, 'in a week.' Into this room I was shut, and found
in it, standing by the fire, without any form, the king,
queen, three princesses, and this bedchamber-woman
whoever she was, for I have not made her out, but liked
her very much, because she seemed to like me. It is
impossible for words to express the kind and companion-
able good-humour of the whole party. I almost forgot
that any one of them was my superior. The king
looked fifteen years younger, and much better in the
face, though as red as ever. He said a number of
excellent things, and in the most natural way. The

queen, with amazing address and cleverness, gave a turn
to the conversation, and mixed in it just at the right
places.   You will not believe me when I tell you that
I passed half an hour, at least, in the room.

" The princesses looked as they always do, the pink of
good-humour.   The Princess Royal had a very fine
colour, the two others were pale.   The king did a very
odd thing by the Princess Royal ; but I loved him for
it.   He said, ' he would ask me, as a man of taste, what
I thought of the ceiling ? ' and then called upon the
Princess Royal to explain the allegorical figures on the
ceiling, which she did, blushing a little at first in the
sweetest manner, with a distinct voice, and great
propriety in her emphasis.   This one trait would of
itself demonstrate how very kind they were.   The king
began by asking me ' how I could run away from
London, and give up my fees ? '   I told him that I *never*
minded fees, but *less* when they interfered with my sense
of duty to him.   The queen then came up to me, and
said, ' You have less merit in the visit, because a little
bird has told me that you are on your way to your
circuit.'

" We then went slap-dash into politics, queen and all.
The king laughed heartily at the rats, by that name, and
said, ' they were the boldest rats he ever knew, for that
all the calculation was against them.   Even —— said
It was probable I should recover : not that I am recovered,
according to *some* of them : and yet I have read the last
report of the physicians, which is tolerably good proof

that I am well. By the way, your uncle is considerably
better, and I flatter myself that *my* getting well has done
him good.' I then said, that I had left him in some
alarm how he was to wear the Windsor uniform, with
a tie wig over it, from the fear that he should be mistaken
for an old general that had fought at the battle of
Dettingen. The queen said, 'Oh! I plead guilty to
that ; and I see you enjoy it. I said Hardinge will
enjoy it; for though he is very good-natured, he loves a
little innocent mischief.' The king then told me the
whole story of the conference with Pitt; commended the
House of Commons, and said, 'his illness had in the end
been a perfect bliss only to him, as proving to him how
nobly the people would support him when he was
confined.' This tempted me to say that it was no
political debate, but the contest between generous
humanity and mean cruelty, and it interested human
nature. Then we talked of Mrs. Siddons, Jordan, &c.,
and the queen said, 'Siddons was going to Germany,
to make the English find out by her absence that she
was good for something.' Then we flew to Handel;
after which the king made me a most gracious bow and
said, 'I am going to my dinner'; on which he withdrew."

There was a young *protégé* named Griffith, whom she
desired to recommend to the patronage of Bishop Hurd.
Who would imagine that a queen would address her
request so modestly and in such " bated " fashion as this ?
Totally relying on your goodness that, in case he

should, after inquiry, not be found what he ought to be, you will forget the application entirely."

The queen always took a deep and practical interest in the matter of Sunday schools. The philanthropic Mr. Raikes, whose figure, arrayed in quaint Georgian costume, is now to be seen on the Embankment, was at this time pressing his great system forward ; and her Majesty was eager to hear the details from his own lips. He accordingly came to Windsor and explained to her all his project. She was greatly interested, and, on taking leave, assured him that she envied those who had the power of doing so much good, by the agency of their own personal spirit and agency. There was another advocate of his system, the excellent Mrs. Trimmer, of Brentford, who also excited the queen's interest : she also was invited to Windsor, in November, 1786. The worthy lady wrote to a friend that " she had inexpressible pleasure in her sensible, humane and truly Christian conversation." The queen took up the Sunday-school project warmly, and gave a practical proof of her interest by founding one at Windsor.

All the queen's familiars were chosen with much judgment. They were rather friends than attendants. Such was Lord Courtown, who is described as " well bred and pleasing ; " the faithful Harcourts, who served her with much devotion; the learned Bryant, the attached Mr. Smelt ; Dr. Herschel, Dr. Lind and many more.

The queen, benevolent as she was, was not at all indiscriminate in her charities, or likely to be imposed

upon. Nothing was given without proper inquiries and
due deliberation. An officer's widow petitioned for aid,
urging that she was left with twelve children to support.
Her Majesty sent a confidential agent to inquire, and
finding the statement true, actually took all the twelve
children in order to be educated and maintained at her
expense. Some time after she learned that the lady had
married again, and to a person who was very well off;
upon which the twelve children were sent back to enjoy
their mother's care.

There is a pleasing scene, a photograph almost, of the
easy, unaffected and affectionate relation of the royal
pair to each other. The king once entered her room
when she was dressing, with some letters in his hand,
and *sans façon* began at once explaining the business
to her, speaking very fast and in German. She was
pleased and agitated with the news, and attempted to
kiss his hand, he did the same to hers, then offered his
cheek. All which passed in presence of her attendant,
as though no one were by. Next moment they began
speaking English, having done with the confidential
matter.

The queen conscientiously devoted all pains and attention to arraying herself for her drawing-rooms, but was
ever delighted to get back into her ordinary dress. We
can see from Gainsborough's fine portrait of her in the
National Portrait Gallery, how sumptuously she could robe
herself, and the dress is no less a marvel of the painter's
technique than an evidence of the elaborate system of

decoration in vogue. She would expatiate on the ease
and comfort of a garment then in fashion known as the
Great Coat. " How I could compose a poem on a Great
Coat," she would exclaim.[1]

Occasionally Mrs. Siddons was brought down to read
for the queen and court, and Fanny was deputed to
welcome and take care of the great tragic actress. She
comported herself in a stately fashion. Fanny found her
stiff; her conversation "formal, sententious and dry."
She read the "Provoked Husband " in a deep, drag-
ging voice. It is curious to find she was received in a
rather cold and formal style—as a performer, in short.
The palace rule on such occasions was always strict
enough and a rigid etiquette enforced. She could
hardly have been pleased.

Sometimes a paragraph got into the papers about Miss
Burney's doings or intentions. She was writing a story—
chronicle of court life—or she was going to resign and be
promoted to a post about the princesses. This threw
her into a delicate distress ; while her companions
maliciously whispered and gossiped. Like Mr. Crummles
she "wondered who put these things into the papers."

---

[1] The lively Fanny was adroit enough to attempt to gain her mistress's
favour by some obsequious lines on this article of apparel of her mistress :

THE GREAT COAT.

Thrice honoured robe ; cannot thou espy
    The form that deigns to show thy worth,
Hear the mild voice, view the arch eye
    That call thy panegyric forth.

These were graciously received.

She fancied that all eyes were on her. She was the
heroine of the court. The queen, who did not quite
relish these histrionics, was suspicious. Fanny went to
her, and made a sort of heroic speech. They little knew
her who could suppose that leaving her Majesty would
be promotion for her. The queen said kindly, " I do
not take it ill, I assure you." Fanny went on, " Far
from having any wish for it, your Majesty does not bestow a smile upon me that does not secure my attachment," compliments that were out of place and not in the
best taste. The queen answered her with a smile and
a condescending little bow, " You are very good " ;
there was here possibly a touch of irony.

It was in March, 1789, that the fair Fanny had a
regular battle royal with Mrs. Schwellenberg on the score
of having a window in the carriage up. The old German
dame had by this time been much exasperated by Miss
Burney's want of respect and open dislike to her, and,
possibly to annoy her, insisted on the window being kept
down, in a bitter wind. The other submitted, and contracted a feverish cold, which much " pulled her down,"
though she attended to her duties, which she performed
" with a difficulty all but insurmountable." Her appearance, of course, drew some questions from the queen.
Fanny saw that her Majesty thought "she had been guilty
of some imprudence," but she simply told her the story
of the window-glass without making any complaint. The
prudent lady, who by this time had come thoroughly
to know, even *approfondir* her Fanny, showed some

surprise, "You would hardly catch cold from so slight a cause." With Mrs. Delany she had often the window down? The young lady answered rather pertly, "No, ma'am, nor will Mrs. Locke—nor will Mrs. Thrale, but they left me the regulating of the glass on my own side." Most probably Mrs. Schwellenberg had given her version ; anyhow, her Majesty was not sympathetic.

It is surprising that no one has taken Miss Burney in hand, by way of illustrating a display of character and weakness which exceeds even that of Bozzy himself. It is apparent that she was quite unconscious that she was causing genuine amusement to the whole *entourage*, to whom all her little exhibitions of self-complacent vanity were but too visible, yet a good-natured allowance was made in return for the entertainment she furnished. It is plain that almost every transaction she describes was mistaken by her, and that she magnified or distorted the share she took in them.

At last her Majesty gave her a good-natured hint which anyone less vain and frivolous would have taken.

" This morning, while her hair was dressing, my royal mistress suddenly said, ' Did you see anybody yesterday?' I could not but be sure of her meaning, and though vexed to be anticipated in my avowal, I instantly answered, ' Yes, ma'am ; Mr. Smelt in the morning, and Mr. Fairly in the evening.' ' Oh ! Mr. Fairly was here, then ? ' I was now doubly sorry she should know this only from me ! A little while after,—' Did he go away from you early ? ' she said. ' No, ma'am,' I immedi.

ately answered, 'not early ; he drank tea with me, as
he generally does, I believe, when he is here for the
night.' 'Perhaps,' cried she after a pause, 'the gentleman below do not drink tea.' 'I cannot tell, ma'am, I
never heard him say ; I only knew he asked me if I would
give him some, and I told him yes, with great pleasure.' "

We can admire here the good-natured forbearance of
the queen and her delicate fashion of conveying her
wishes.   A more plain-spoken sovereign would have
simply directed that Miss Burney should change her
methods.

The Colonel, however, continued his visits in his
favourite mysterious way, Fanny receiving him, and
paying no attention to the queen's wishes.

"While the Queen's hair was rolling up, by the wardrobe
woman, at night, Mrs. Schwellenberg happened to leave
the room, and almost instantly her Majesty, in a rather
abrupt manner, said, 'Is Mr. Fairly here to-night?'
'Yes, ma'am.' 'When did he come back?' I could
not recollect. 'I did not know he was here !' 'I knew,
indeed,' she then added, ' he was here in the morning
but I understood he went away afterwards.'

" The idea of connivance now struck me with a real
disdain, that brought back my courage and recollection
in full force, and I answered, 'I remember, ma'am, he
told me he had rode over to Richmond Park at noon,
and returned here to dinner with Colonel Welbred, and
in the evening he drank tea with me, and said he should
sup with General Harcourt.'

" All this, spoken with an openness that rather invited than shunned further investigation, seemed to give an immediate satisfaction ; the tone of voice changed to its usual complacency, and she inquired various things concerning the Stuart family, and then spoke upon more common topics. I concluded it now all over ; but soon after Mrs. Sandys went away, and then, very unexpectedly the queen renewed the subject. ' The reason,' she said, ' that I asked about Mr. Fairly was that the Schwellenberg sent to ask Miss Planta to come to her, because Mr. Fairly was —no, not with her—he never goes to her.' She stopped ; but I was wholly silent. I felt instantly with how little propriety I could undertake either to defend or to excuse Mr. Fairly, whom I determined to consider as a visitor, over whom, having no particular influence, I could be charged with no particular responsi- bility. After waiting a few minutes—' With you,' she said, ' Mr Fairly was and the Schwellenberg was alone.'

" The inward conflict silenced me from saying any- thing else.

" I believe she was surprised ; but she added, after a long pause, ' I believe—he comes to you every evening when here ? '

" ' I do not know, ma'am, always, when he is here or away ; but I am always very glad to see him, for indeed his visits make all the little variety that—' (An extra- ordinary reproach to make in the presence of her Majesty.)

"She immediately took up the word, but without the slightest displeasure. 'Why here there might be more variety than anywhere, from the nearness to town, except for—'

"' The present situation of things,' I eagerly interrupted her to say, and went on :—'Indeed, ma'am, I have scarce a wish to break into the present arrangement, by seeing anybody while the house is in this state ; nor have I, from last October, seen one human being that does not live here, except Mr. Smelt, Mr. Fairly, and Sir Lucas Pepys ; and they all come upon their own calls, and not for me.' ' The only objection,' she gently answered, 'to seeing anybody, is that every one who comes carries some sort of information away with them.' I assured her I was perfectly content to wait for better times. Here the matter dropped ; she appeared satisfied with what I said, and became soft and serene as before the little attack."

There has been a great deal of misconception as to the causes of Miss Burney's giving up her situation at court, chiefly owing to her own very vivacious, but rather partial and over-coloured account. This piece of pleading has enlisted general sympathy and indignation, as she seemed to hold herself out as the victim of oppressive court routine and servitude. The little scenes just given show very clearly that it was impossible she could remain much longer. Her free and easy behaviour, her high opinion of herself and of her talents, made her fancy that she was a privileged person and independent of all rule. What

chiefly led to her departure was the rather intolerable
amount of these flirtations, which were quite indiscriminate and led to disorder, and the neglect of duties.
But I am inclined to believe that the more immediate
cause of her resignation was the mortification consequent
on her failure to capture " Mr. Fairly," alias the
Honourable Colonel Digby, at whom she had been
" setting her cap " so openly and recklessly as to defy
public opinion and become the general talk of the
palace.   When this gentleman " threw her over " without warning, the situation and the ridicule of her position
could not be faced.

During the crisis of the king's malady, the " goings
on " with this Colonel, the readings of poetry together in
private chambers, the secrecy and surprises, the hiding
of the book as someone intruded on the pair—all these
things were but portions of the attack which the fair
Fanny carried on in the boldest fashion.   It did seem
that, for a time at least, the gentleman *had* " intentions."
In the household there were sly jests, " nods and becks,"
at what was going on ; the queen, too, was aware of it,
and could not approve of her lady's duties being neglected
or " scamped " in this fashion.

It came to November of the year 1789—and the date
should be noted carefully in this matter—when she was
somewhat taken aback by a jocose remark of Colonel
Gwynn's that his friend Fairly had a fit of the gout, but
that " he had a nurse in view."   The queen had spoken
of him with some severity for spreading a false report

about the drawing-room. Miss Burney defended him
when her Majesty said, somewhat sharply, that *he had
reasons* for coming there : "How I was amazed and
'silenced,'" she writes. A day or two later she was told
the news—"Mr. Fairly was going to be married !"—but
she did not believe it. But alas ! on January 6th, 1790,
he *was* married to Miss Gunning, "Miss Fuzileer," who
had been all the time quietly carrying on her operations.
And a week later the pair came to see her, whom she
received very ruefully.

Presently, in May, when her brother pressed her to
speak to the queen about his advancement—a proceeding quite against the rules and often forbidden—we find
that she had made up her mind to retire, and adds most
significantly, "*while I may*." This shows she had
determined to leave, and I think proves the immediate
connection between her public mortification and her
withdrawal. She now opened the matter to her father,
and began to draw up her memorial of resignation, but
lingered on for the rest of the year. And there may
have been another motive at work. This egregious flirt
had really attracted the admiration of Windham, the
popular and brilliant statesman, and who distinguished
her with the most flattering attentions. It is plain that
she had hopes of capturing him. But unluckily the only
opportunities were found at the Hastings trial. How
could she bring the affair to any issue, when cooped up
and imprisoned in the palace ? Once free, and in her
father's circle, there would be plenty of openings. This

was certainly in her mind. Her health, too, it may be admitted, was not good.

Mrs. Papendieck has a curious story as to this resignation—which, however, may be the gossip of the palace. It was reported that she had written a third novel, and had asked the queen to read it and allow its dedication to her. This was refused as the queen would not sanction novel-writing under her own roof. It would lead, she thought, " to a want of cheerful and pleasant attendance," and she felt certain that when she rang, " the pen would be laid down with regret and duty be found irksome." This seems probable enough, though Miss Burney naturally does not mention it. She would, of course, have been eager to come once before the public and receive applause : while the queen would as naturally dislike the idea of a novel being published as it were from her own house. There was also, as we have seen, a belief that she was busy sketching off the characters about her, and her voluminous diaries which must have taken a great deal of her time to keep " posted up," cannot have escaped the notice of the servants and courtiers ; they would go about repeating that Miss Burney was at work " putting them all into a book." Nor is it unlikely even that a glimpse of these amusing and personal records may have been obtained ; a danger of which the fair authoress was not unconscious, as she affected to disguise her characters under fictitious names.

She felt, however, very nervous when the time came

for opening the matter to her royal mistress. She drew
up a solemn "memorial," which she long hesitated to
present. At last the plunge was made. There is something highly characteristic, dramatic even, in the rage
and fury of the old Schwellenberg, who though glad
to be rid of an enemy, resented comically enough this
outrage to all court traditions and feeling. She expos-
tulated as though the step led to destruction, as though
life itself removed from the palace walls became an evil.

But the resignation dragged on. The queen, who
delighted in the progress of the Hastings trial, and liked
Miss Burney's lively descriptions of it, now wanted her
to attend regularly and report to her. The young lady
declined on the plea that her health being known as the
cause of her retirement, people would remark her appearance at a place of entertainment; "reports might be
spread." The good queen accepted this odd excuse. Nay,
when she sent her to bed on a ball night, and had someone
else to sit up for her, Miss Burney rather ungraciously
told her Majesty that this favour made her the more feel
the necessity of her retreat, as it proved that her place
ought to be supplied by one who could better perform
her office. " She was not much pleased with this speech."

Mrs. Schwellenberg, as I have said, was aghast at the
news ; she thought it led to destruction, and offered to
save her from the awful consequences. She took the
paper to the queen, who, though much astonished, good-
naturedly proposed that Fanny should go to the country
for six weeks to get better. In time the queen asked

after her health : " Are you not a little better—not a little—not a little bit ? "   But Fanny was resolved.

Nothing could be more affectionately gracious than the behaviour of the queen and royal family to their departing servant.   There could not be anything very acceptable in the step Miss Burney was taking.   Reasonable as it was, it seemed a slight ; for the posts about the court were so eagerly sought and devotion to the family so much a matter of duty, it seemed that to enter into their service was to become theirs until death.   Yet here was this clever young lady departing from the court under a sense of grievance and disgust, and conveying plainly that the service was unendurable.

The generous liberality of the queen was displayed in an extraordinary way.   The young lady, who took on herself all the airs of a sacrificed heroine, even ventured to suggest arrangements for her successor, Mademoiselle Jacobi, whom she scarcely knew ; urging that a young relation should be treated, not as a servant, but as her companion.   This the good-natured queen listened to " with humane complacency."   She treated her munificently ; promised her two hundred a year from her own purse.   She had her handkerchief to her eyes during the whole time of the farewell.   The king came into the room to say good-bye, but seeing she was affected and kept her face turned away from him, with much delicacy quitted the room.

" They all were now going.   I took, for the last time, the cloak of the Queen, and, putting it over her shoulders, slightly ventured to press them, earnestly saying, though in a low voice, 'God Almighty bless your Majesty!' She turned round, and, putting her hand upon my ungloved arm, pressed it with the greatest kindness, and said, 'May you be happy!'

"She left me overwhelmed with tender gratitude. The three eldest Princesses were in the next room : they ran in to me the moment the Queen went onward. Princess Augusta and Princess Elizabeth each took a hand, and the Princess Royal put hers over them. I could speak to none of them ; but they repeated, 'I wish you happy! —I wish you health!' again and again, with the sweetest eagerness. They then set off for Kew. Here, therefore, end my Court Annals ; after having lived in the service of Her Majesty five years within ten days— from July 17th, 1786, to July 7th, 1791." Such was Fanny Burney's leave-taking. It seems likely that in her later troubles and difficulties she must have often regretted the foolish and precipitate step she had taken.

After a long interval, and when Fanny had made her improvident marriage with a penniless French emigrant, M. d'Arblay, the queen did not lose sight of her, but even treated her with the greatest kindness and consideration. She received her, and even allowed her on occasions to attend her.

"The Queen was in her White Closet, working at a round table, with the four remaining Princesses, Augusta, Mary, Sophia, and Amelia. She received me most sweetly, and with a look of far better spirits than upon my last admission. She permitted me, in the most gracious manner, to inquire about the Princess Royal, now Duchess of Wurtemberg.

" The Princesses Mary and Amelia had a little opening between them ; and when the Queen was conversing with some lady who was teaching the Princess Sophia some work, they began a whispering conversation with me about my little boy. How tall is he ?—how old is he ?—is he fat or thin ?—is he like you or M. d'Arblay ? &c., &c.—with sweet vivacity of interest,—the lovely Princess Amelia finishing her listening to my every answer with a 'dear little thing !' that made me long to embrace her as I have done in her childhood. She is now full as tall as Princess Royal, and as much formed ; she looks seventeen, though only fourteen, but has an innocence, an Hebe blush, an air of modest candour, and a gentleness so caressingly inviting, of voice and eye, that I have seldom seen a more capitvating young creature. The Queen, catching the domestic theme, presently made inquiries herself, as to M. d'Arblay and the child, asking, with respect to the latter, ' Is he here ? ' as if she meant in the palace. I told her I had come so unexpectedly myself upon my father's difficulties, that I had not this time brought my little shadow. I believed, however, I should fetch him, as if I lengthened mv stay, M. d'Arblay would come also. ' To be sure !' she said, as if feeling the trio's full objections to separating."

CHAPTER XII.

By March, 1791, a sort of reconciliation had been brought about between the prince and his royal mother. "A gentleman," wrote Walpole, humorously, "who lives at the end of St. James's Park has been sent for by a lady who has a large house at the West-end, and they have kissed and are friends, which he notified by my toasting her health in a bumper at a club the other day." In spite of an occasional coldness, this queen, in the interest of herself and her family, seemed henceforward to strive to keep on good terms with her eldest son : a prudent course, as it was likely she would soon have no other protector to look to.

On November 23rd in this year their Majesties' second son, the Duke of York, was married to the eldest daughter of the King of Prussia, at the queen's desire. This was the most important of all the alliances that were made by the royal family during the period of some sixty or seventy years that was to follow : until the era of that even more auspicious marriage of the Princess Royal of our time with the eldest son of the

King of Prussia. The Duchess of York proved to be a
staid and prudent princess, though she was destined to
be much tried by the extravagance of her husband,
under which she bore herself with firmness and becoming
resignation. Her warm heart attached to her a circle of
friends; as can be seen from the generous testimony
furnished by that thorough man of the world, Mr.
Charles Greville. In her later years she exhibited some
oddities—notably, a passion for dogs—but her retreat
from the world and secluded life at Weybridge was
no doubt owing to disgust at the wild disorders and
general recklessness of the regent's court.

As though the troubles pressing on the royal family
were not sufficient, their children contrived to contribute
as far as they could to the anxieties of their parents. As
the papers put it, there was "one circumstance which
tended to perplex the mind of his Majesty at this
juncture." Prince Augustus met at Rome the two attractive daughters of Lord Dunmore, and eventually married
one, the Lady Augusta Murray. This illegal contract
became a source of great annoyance to the court. The
king promptly instituted a suit in the Court of Arches,
and it was annulled. As there were children of the
marriage, the king was disturbed by constantly-recurring
claims for recognition, and the name of Sir Augustus
D'Este was very often before the public.

Indeed, it seemed to be the destiny of this afflicted
family that even the ordinary incidents of family life,
which are hailed as fortunate blessings, such as marriages,

birth of children and the like, were in this case to be new elements of misery. His eldest son's well-known secret or illegal marriage, had been a sore trouble, and the father and mother might fairly congratulate themselves on at last "fixing him" when they induced him to consent to a desirable alliance. Yet on the wedding-day itself—when the prince, in disgust, called for "Harris" to get him a glass of brandy—this dream was at once dissolved, and the ill-starred pair began that scandalous quarrel which was to last for over thirty years.

The stages of the struggle are familiar, with its "delicate investigation," courts of inquiry into conduct, battles over the child, claim to be received at court, all which must have added to the queen's worries. Many and many must have been the agitating family councils held at the palace to settle what was to be done with this plague, for some course had to be settled on in dealing with the perverse and erratic lady, who was not to be put aside. Nor was this all. As the little Princess Charlotte grew up, it was plain that she could not be educated fitly in a household where the father pursued his pleasures without restraint and the mother lay under the gravest suspicions. Hence arose a fresh chapter of troubles and disorders. The unlucky selection that had been made was eventually to confront them with new difficulties, for it was before them either to take part with their son against his wife or with the wife against their son. In the early days the Princess of Wales found kind and affectionate protectors in the royal family, who did all they could to atone for the neglect and ill-treatment of her husband. But soon her own indiscretions, the scandals of the " delicate investigations," " the book," etc., deprived her of this protection.

The details of this unhappy business properly belong to the history of the king's reign, and of his son's regency and reign.[1] The queen was but little concerned in these matters. A person so correct and strict in her manners was not likely to relish such a daughter-in-law. It was not until the regency and the final effacement of the king that she departed from her cold neutrality and openly took part with her son.

The birth and education of the little Princess Charlotte produced a great dispute between the king and son as to who should have charge of her education, for her mother was admittedly an unsuitable person. There was much unpleasant wrangling on this matter. The king and queen offered to be at all the charges of her bringing up ; but her father would only consent on terms that would be advantageous to himself. He yielded at last to their persuasions or pressure, but almost as soon as he had agreed drew back from his engagement. He even denied that he had made such an engagement, on the pretence that he did not know that the king's mind was affected at the time. At last conditions of his own interest induced him to give way, and this charming child, then about eleven years old, came under the

[1] They are set forth at length in the author's " Life of George the Fourth."

direction of her grandparents. Indeed, this little Princess Charlotte was one of the quaintest and most remarkable children ; everything she did or said had " character" and was strikingly original. For instance, when only nine years old she made this remark on reading the second chapter of St. Matthew : "I think," says she, "Joseph ought not to have been afraid of returning into Judæa when God told him by an angei he might return ; but I leave that to be settled by the Bishop of London."

When only three years old she received the grave Mrs. Hannah Moore, took her by the hand, showed her all her little properties, and ended by reciting " The Busy Bee," performing a dance, and singing " God save the King!" Most of the princesses when children exhibited something striking ; witness that speech of the little Princess Mary, who, having forgotten Mrs. Delany's name, advanced in a cherry-coloured *tablier* with silver strings, and greeted her : "How do you do, *Duchess of Portland's friend?* How does your little niece do? I wish you had brought her." This was as quaint as it was clever. The little Charlotte used to say in her odd fashion, " There are two things that I do not like at all : one is apple tart, and the' other is my grandmother." Yet the queen was truly fond of her, nervously concerned for her health and interest, but she had the German notion of strict discipline for girls. What could be more affectionate than this letter, written in 1808 ?

THE QUEEN TO LADY DE CLIFFORD.

Though I am certain, my dear Lady de Clifford, that you will inform us every day what progress dear little Charlotte is making in her present disagreeable complaint, I cannot resist writing a few lines to inquire after her, and to desire you will assure the dear child how very sincerely we interest ourselves here in her speedy recovery. I cannot possibly wish her better than that she may get on as smoothly as dear Amelia, who got through the measles without any drawback whatever, and she would now be out if the great delicacy of her chest did not make particular quiet and care necessary. You, madam, who have been witness to so many disorders in children, of course must know that this complaint requires particular care ; and I must name one thing in general little regarded, and yet of the utmost consequence, which is that of changing the linen too early. As you are a great friend to James's powder, I am sure you will not prevent its being given, as it is of great assistance in forwarding the distemper : it did so with dear Amelia . . . I trust you do not suspect me of disturbing either your zeal or attention upon this occasion, that would be doing you the greatest injustice : but my head *is so full of fears and dangers of late*, that when the heart is full it will come out with whatever is uppermost. Nor do I mean to question Sir W. F.'s (Sir W. Farquhar) skill. I have only to add how sincerely I wish that you may not suffer yourself, from your anxiety, and that your grand-

children may either escape or get well through this
complaint. Pray do not offend Sir W. F. with what I
have wrote. Excuse the anxiety of a grandmother."

About the year 1797 it was known that there was a
marriage on the *tapis* for one of the young princesses, and
the Prince of the duchy of Wurtemburg, who was heir to
the sovereignty, had offered his hand to the princess royal.
His family was connected with that of the queen, and the
match was thought a desirable one. It seemed odd
indeed that these fair young princesses had not before
now been mated, the princess royal being now past
thirty. There were, however, some grave incidents in
the history of this prince, which made this connection
scarcely suitable. He had been a widower some nine
years, having been married to one of the Brunswick
princesses, with whom was associated one of those extraordinary mysteries which seemed to attend the reign
of Catherine of Russia. The princess was no more than
sixteen and her husband was ten years older. After
the marriage the prince entered the Russian service, his
sister being married to the heir-apparent of that empire.
" On going to Petersburgh, he took his wife and three
children with him ; and the princess being then in the
flower of her youth, of a lively disposition, and fascinating
manners, soon became a favourite with the Empress
Catherine, whose court and company were far from being
favourable to the morals. In that vortex of dissipation,
however, the prince imprudently allowed his wife to be
drawn, and leaving her behind him when he made his

campaign against the Turks. On his return he found her principles undermined and contaminated, and her conduct the subject of general observation. In this situation he wrote to her father, the Duke of Brunswick, informing him of his daughter's behaviour, and requesting his advice. The result of this correspondence was a resolution that she should be removed out of Russia ; and the prince accordingly demanded leave of the empress to quit her dominions with his family. Catherine readily allowed the prince the permission he requested, as far as related to himself and his children, but refused to allow the princess to return to Germany. No remonstrances could induce her to recede from her determination, and the prince, with his sons and daughter, quitted the Russian territories for Wirtemberg. About a fortnight after their departure the princess was sent by an imperial order to the Castle Lhorde, about two hundred miles from Petersburgh, having been first deprived of all her German attendants ; and before the expiration of two years the prince received a letter from the empress, informing him of the death of his wife, similar information being sent to the duke her father. As is always the case in such dark transactions, there were not wanting sceptics who called in question the veracity of the empress, and would not believe the account which she gave of the death of the princess. Many persons in Germany tenaciously maintained that she was still living in a state of confinement, or an exile in Siberia ; and this was the constant opinion of the late Duchess of Bruns-

wick, her mother, although her husband and brother
were satisfied to the contrary.

"When, therefore, the hereditary prince made an offer
of his hand to the Princess Royal of England, the king
was much affected, and more so on perceiving that the
overture met with a favourable reception on the part of
his daughter. Having before his eyes the tragical
narrative of his unfortunate relative, as far as it was
known, he felt an extreme repugnance to the proffered
alliance, nor was the queen less averse to it ; but their
joint remonstrances were of no avail, nor could even the
fate of her cousin deter the princess from giving an assent
to the proposal. Her royal father, however, deemed it
necessary to make a very close inquiry into the particulars
that had been just detailed, before he gave his final
answer ; and having ascertained the fact of the death of
the Princess of Wirtemberg in Russia, his consent was
no longer withheld.

"His Majesty hesitated, and waited till the last moment
for the final decision of the princess, when finding that
her determination was irrevocably fixed, he said no more ;
and the union took place with circumstances of great
pomp at the Chapel Royal in the afternoon of the
18th of May. The service was performed by the
Archbishop of Canterbury, with the assistance of his
Grace of York, his Majesty giving away the bride ; in
doing which the whole audience observed how greatly he
was agitated, while the queen and the other princesses
appeared overpowered with sorrow. When the religious

service in the chapel was concluded, her Majesty held a
drawing-room, which was numerously attended ; and on
breaking up, the whole of the royal family, with the
Prince and Princess of Wirtemberg, left town for Windsor
Lodge."

The future bride was at this time suffering from jaun-
dice, and when she appeared at the drawing-room in
February, a lynx-eyed observer noted that there was
still " a light tinge of the disorder round her eyes." The
prince did not arrive in London until a very short time
before the marriage.[1]

Among the many trials of the queen—and never was a
poor lady of high position subjected to such a variety of
ingeniously varied agitations—was that of the constantly
recurring attempts at assassinating her husband. She
never knew the moment when news would be brought to
her of some fresh attempt: madwomen or madmen often
went near to effecting their purpose. Familiar is the
story of the attempt by Margaret Nicholson, one of this
class, and of the good-natured expedition of the Spanish
minister, Del Campo, to prepare the queen. Miss Burney
has described the sufferings of the whole family, their

[1] Meantime the usual handsome presents had been offered, among
others a superb diamond ring of thirty brilliants. By an odd fatality,
as the ornament was being made by Forster, the court jeweller, a chicken
somehow got into the workshop and literally pecked out and swallowed
all the stones one by one. It was fortunately caught in the act of dispos-
ing of the last, when it was promptly put to death, and all the stones
recovered from its gizzard ! Odd adventures like this were constantly
recurring, and show the easy, "happy-go-lucky" principles of the
system after which things royal were carried on.

THE ELDER PRINCESSES
(1785).

tears, which could not be restrained for weeks after, and the coolness of the king. The queen was with him when the pistol was fired at him in the theatre, in February, 1796. She was driving with him through the streets when a stone was thrown at them through the carriage window. "It was a smooth flint," says Miss Holroyd, "cut into sharp corners, that was flung. It touched the queen's cheek. The king caught it in his hand, and gave it to Lord Harrington, who was in the carriage, to 'keep for his sake.' The Duchess of Newcastle mentioned this."

It was a favourite topic with the scurrilous jesters of the time, that penuriousness and stinginess reigned at the palace. The notorious Peter Pindar indulged in much coarse ridicule of this kind, and certainly presented his Majesty under grotesque forms and conditions. Even the wits of the Rolliad were pleasant on the subject :—

> " Fall to, ye royal crew !
> Eat ! eat ! your bellies full—pray do—
> At treats I never winces ;
> The queen shall say
> Once in a way,
> Her maids have been well crammed—
> Her young ones dined like princes ! "

The poor Schwellenberg and her general greed was a favourite topic with Peter :—

> " Sooner shall Madam Schwellenberg, the jade,
> Yield up her favourite perquisites of trade,
> Give up her sacred Majesty's old gowns,
> Caps, petticoats and aprons, without frowns.
> She ! who for ever studies mischief—she !
> Who will soon be busy as a bee—

She ! who hath got more insolence and pride—
God mend her heart !—than half the world beside—
She ! who of guttling fond, stuffs down more meat—
Heaven help her stomach !—than ten men can eat ! "

It is astonishing that such gross scurrility could be tolerated.

One of the boldest of Walcot's productions was a coarse pasquinale called " The Lousiad," founded on an incident which was said to have occurred at one of the royal suppers.   It could not be denied, however, that the doctor showed a good deal of fun and satire in his task of ridiculing the court, and particularly the king; and as the public read and laughed, he never relaxed in his efforts.   Some green peas had been served to his Majesty, who, looking closely, detected a hair.   This discovery caused a perfect commotion in the palace, and serious indignation among the higher powers, and after a solemn investigation, it was actually decreed that all cooks, scullions, and *tutti quanti*, should have their heads shaved as a qualification for office—an injudicious proceeding which caused much discussion, and was considered to touch the liberty of the subject.   Strange to say, the doctor eventually received a pension, which his enemies contended was what he had in view all along.

Indeed, these attacks of Peter Pindar seem to have been mainly accountable for the stories that were circulated of the queen's penuriousness and saving ways.   As we have seen, a more truly liberal lady there could not be.   Her hand was always open for distress ; but she had the thrift of her country, could not tolerate waste, and wished to have full value for what she laid out. A characteristic story was circulated, which shows how her liberal acts could be distorted. A Weymouth linen-draper offered for sale a quantity of calico at a low price —sixpence a yard. The queen learning of the bargain, sent at once and purchased the whole *en bloc*. A cry was raised that the queen had interfered with the poorer Weymouth folk, and prevented them from getting a "good thing," and the tradesman grumbled because payment was delayed till the other accounts were settled. There was no doubt something injudicious in her purchase, for such comments might have been antici-pated; but as it turned out, the larger portion was given away to the poor, though some was reserved for cutting up into chair covers.[1]

---

[1] The scale of her subscriptions was almost magnificent ; £500 a year to a needlework society ; £200 a year to a school, &c. Her "stand-ing" list on pensions to servants, charities, &c., was over £5000 a year.

CHAPTER XIII.

FAMILY TROUBLES—PRINCESS CHARLOTTE.

ONE of the most disastrous results of the recurring malady of the king was the change it produced in the relations of members of the royal family to each other. After the long and serious attack of 1789 the illnesses began to return at intervals; and any crisis or agitation, as the family came to learn, caused intense anxiety, as they knew it was the forerunner of one of his seizures. It may be said, indeed, that from that date the king's reason was permanently unsettled, though he enjoyed long intervals of the kind that were called "lucid." Connected with the affection were the well-known eccentricities of speech and manner, the volubility of talk, the recurring "What? What?" which was so much ridiculed, in ignorance of the unhappy cause, and constant changes of scene. The admirable queen and her excellent daughters had thus the whole current of their pleasing domestic life altered; a weight of anxiety pressed on them, and they watched with feverish interest every sign that could betoken the approach of the fatal malady. By an unfortunate concatenation a number of harassing events were constantly exciting the unfortunate monarch—the most serious ministerial difficulties, such as the loss of Mr. Pitt; the having persons like Mr. Fox, whose principles he loathed, forced upon him; the pressure of the Catholic claims, which he regarded with a morbid horror. But the most serious affliction of all was his undutiful treatment by his eldest son, who, he knew, was acting as his declared enemy, and even eagerly striving to thrust him from his place.

In February, 1801, the unhappy queen and her family were disturbed by premonitory symptoms of a return of the king's malady. This was, as usual, brought on by agitation, but more particularly by great carelessness as to taking cold or catching chills. While the fit lasted there were the usual "hurries" and incoherence. One gratifying circumstance was the complete reform in the behaviour of the Duke of York, who devoted himself to his mother and sisters, and separated himself from his elder brother. He was almost worn out by his attendance and watching. The Prince's behaviour was, unfortunately, of the usual kind. Fortunately the malady was of short duration, lasting not longer than three weeks. Not a month later he had a relapse—the attack taking the shape of extreme nervousness.

The Prince of Wales attended, but it was said behaved very rudely to the queen. From this attack, however, the king once more rallied.

By the year 1804 the queen, whose own nerves had

been shaken by the dread of the malady, had begun to regard, almost with terror, the wild and sometimes frantic displays to which her unhappy partner gave way, and dreaded now to trust herself in his company, even in his saner moments. His morose sensitiveness was roused by this conduct. She persisted in living entirely separate— she fancied, and perhaps had reason to do so, that it was dangerous to be with him, as some sudden paroxysm might seize on him. She would never receive him without one of the princesses ; and would, we are told, "never say in reply a word." Her boudoir door was kept strictly locked against him. He dined by himself at two ; she and her daughters an hour or so later. He was allowed to come in at dessert. The queen, we are told by Lord Malmesbury, piqued herself on this " judicious silence," which might seem to be scarcely judicious, and was only too likely to fortify the evil. But she was a sensible lady, and, there can be little doubt, had good reasons for her course—one of which was certainly the strange talk in which the king would break out, regardless of who might be present. But the result of his ostracism was what might be expected. He deeply resented it, and the once amiable, good-humoured king now began to change into a morose, irritable and suspicious man. He even showed to her a sort of hostility. The princesses naturally ranged themselves on their mother's side. "Within the family," says Lord Auckland, "are strange schisms and cabals, and divisions among his sons and daughters." What inflamed him most was the queen,

on one occasion taking the side of her eldest son—
prudently wishing to conciliate him.

These attempts of the king to assert himself and show
that he had a will of his own often had the result of
throwing the whole household into confusion. He
would capriciously turn off retainers and servants—from
the Chamberlain to the grooms and footmen. The
queen's favourite coachman was dismissed, as well as his
own faithful page, Braun, who had nursed him through
his illness. This added to the worries of the queen,
who, it was noticed, became "cross" and ill. At the
drawing-rooms and other public functions it was
remarked how pale she looked ; and the princesses had
all the tokens of weeping and misery.   Lord Auckland
had heard that the king "never mentions her with disrespect, but he marks unequivocally that he is dissatisfied,
and has come to a decided system of checking her
knowledge of what is going forward and her interference
between him and her son."

The queen's temper in these disastrous circumstances,
as we have seen, was noticed to be "fractious" and rest-
less in the extreme.   "The prince," we are told, "was
highly discontented ; the queen and Princesses Augusta
and Elizabeth, with the Dukes of Clarence, Kent and
Sussex, siding with him ; whilst the Dukes of York,
Cumberland and Cambridge, and the younger princesses,
adhered to the king."   " I am told," it was added, " the
breach every day grows wider."   This explains why
the king allowed of all his family only the two younger

princesses to dine with him, which they did alternately.

At the end of October in this year (1804) the king and his family, after spending some time at his favourite Weymouth, went to stay with his friend Mr. Rose at Cuffnells. He rode a great deal, and talked in a very free and interesting way with his host, relating past incidents in his life. During one of these rides an incident occurred which illustrates in a striking way the characters of the royal family. The young Princess Amelia, who was cantering down a hill, was thrown from her horse, falling on her face. She rose at once, wishing to convey that she was not hurt, but, it was evident, was a good deal shaken.

Naturally she shrank from remounting her horse. But the king, in Roman-father fashion, insisted that she should either get into the carriage and be taken home and bled, or else continue her ride. The high-spirited girl at once chose the latter and mounted, though, when she reached Southampton, she had herself privately blooded. The king explained to his host that " he could not bear that any of his family should want courage," to which his friend urged that a certain care and caution on an accident was barely want of courage. " Perhaps it may be so," was the answer of the king, " but I thank Heaven there is but one of my children that wants courage, and I will not name him because he is to succeed me." There was some truth in his remarkable and pointed statement. The king himself had the most determined and collected courage : so had the queen and her daughters ; they could confront difficulties, trials, and dangers in the most undaunted way ; and nearly all his sons, as he truly said, were distinguished in the same way. In fairness to the Prince of Wales, it should be said that he was of a nervous temperament, and his resolution had been enfeebled by excesses. He was also very vacillating and undecided.

Passing over an interval of some years which is without interest for us, we come to the year 1810, than which nothing could be more disastrous for the poor queen. Upon her head horror upon horrors seemed to accumulate.

By Christmas the king was as bad as ever—often of a night in serious danger. Then set in the old painful incidents—the gathering of the doctors, the sending for Dr. John Willis, and the old battle of conflicting opinions, bulletins, &c., over his unhappy person. A Regency followed as a matter of course, when there was the old contention to make him out better or worse, according to the interests and wishes of the factions. The queen, as before, was to have control of the king, direction of his household, and a council to assist her.

The poor sufferer had always a sort of maniacal horror of Dr. Willis, from the association with his former experience of twenty years before, and he had made the queen solemnly promise him, that if he became again incapacitated, this practitioner, as well as a Doctor Simmons, should never be called in to attend him. The good queen's anxiety to adhere to this promise led to many painful discussions and contentions. But another of the distressing family incidents which seemed inevitably to attend the royal family took place this year. The Duke of Cumberland was one night roused from his slumbers by a violent attack, receiving two cuts, which he strangely fancied was a bat " beating about his head." His valet, Sellis, or Salis, also was discovered with his throat cut and a sword covered with blood. There was a strange and perhaps needless mystery associated with this affair, and all kinds of rumours were circulated. This was owing, no doubt to the unfavourable opinion which was entertained of the duke, whose somewhat violent and uncontrolled character was well known. The matter, however, was left in a curious state of uncertainty, and never cleared up in a satisfactory way. It was, however, another trouble for his family.

The death of the amiable and interesting young Princess Amelia in 1811 was the last stroke that shipwrecked the domestic happiness of the royal family. As is well known, it completely overset what remained of the king's sanity. This engaging young woman, her father's favourite, had always been in indifferent health, which prevented her following her studies with the assiduity of her sisters, but she was still a very accomplished person, fond of music and painting, and it was said that few could equal her on the pianoforte. She was nursed in the most devoted way by her sister, the Princess Mary, and met her early death with

wonderful placidity and resignation. Her little property
she left to the Prince of Wales, as residuary legatee,
who handsomely made it over to Princess Mary, taking
on himself to discharge the various claims, legacies, &c.
It was said that Miss Gascoigne, her personal attendant,
was so affected by her loss that she pined away and died.
The king had her interred as near as possible to the royal
vault, and an inscription was put in St. George's Chapel,
" in testimony of his grateful sense of the beautiful service and attachment of an amiable young woman to
his beloved daughter, whom she survived only three
months." This affectionate inscription seems to support
the story.

By February, 1812, it might be said that the reign of
the good king was virtually over, and a new sovereign on
the throne. It must have been a strange, though not
unexpected, thing for the queen to be thus, as it were,
deposed, for so she was, and reduced to the state and condition of a dowager queen. Her eyes must have often
turned back, looking across the long stretch of fifty event-
ful years, to that far-off day when she first arrived from
her native Strelitz, a young and interesting bride. She
was now an old and afflicted lady, nigh seventy, and there
were ominous signs that even her small remnant of life
was likely to be further devastated by miseries and agitations. As it was, her position of guardian to the king was
made uncomfortable by jealousies and suspicions.

Not less mortifying and painful to her must have been
the formal break up of this once united and domestic

household. Her remaining daughters, now women of mature ages, unwedded, felt, not perhaps unnaturally, that the time had come when they were entitled to their enfranchisement, and eagerly accepted a proposal of their brother's, the Regent, that they should have establishments of their own. They were persons of strong and marked character, Princess Augusta particularly ; they had their own friends, and indeed it was time that they should begin to see life on a larger scale.

Parliament, after adding £10,000 a year to the queen's income, allotted £3000 a year to each of the princesses. They each set up an establishment and appointed one lady-in-waiting : Princess Augusta choosing Miss Onslow, and getting for her the title of Lady ; Princess Elizabeth, the Dowager Lady Rosslyn ; Princess Mary, Lady Isabella Thynne ; and Princess Sophia, Lady Mary Powlett. They took servants and set up equipages, and also announced to their mother their intention of sometimes paying visits to their brothers. All these new and rather simultaneous notions of independence could not have been acceptable to the queen.

Another affliction was now awaiting the unhappy family. The king was menaced with blindness, while the queen was troubled with a gradually increasing weakness in her feet. Yet nothing was relaxed in the way of promoting the social engagements with which she strove to render the lot of those about them, and of the people generally, happier. No royal family ever took such a share in the general pastimes of society or did so much to encourage a species of harmless gaiety. They took their share in all that was going on. Balls, junketings, fêtes, galas, little tea parties and excursions, visits to subjects, reviews, visits to the play—these all went on as usual, in spite of the recurring afflictions. Few people have an idea of the magnificent style in which a court fête was then organized. Nowadays such things follow an established routine, and a court ball causes little or no excitement. But then each entertainment seemed to be a special effort. As when a grand gala was given at Windsor in 1805, we learn that the castle was put into the hands of Mr. Wyatt, the architect ; a service of plate, costing between twenty and thirty thousand pounds, was ordered for the occasion ; rich glass, costing thousands of pounds, was set forth ; while at the supper four tables of massive silver were displayed, with pier glasses whose frames were also of silver, while nothing but gold and silver plate was used—gold for the royal table ; even "the dogs" of the fireplaces were of solid silver. Two hundred and fifty dozen of silver plates were used for the supper. Nor were the guests behind in magnificence. Many of the nobility came down in their coaches and six. The fair dames almost generally displayed ostrich plumes, eight or nine to cover the head, with jewels of the most costly kind.

In May, all the arrangements for giving the queen charge of the king had been made. These were on a handsome and liberal scale. He was to have his privy purse of £60,000 a year, with an addition of £60,000 a year. The queen received an addition of £10,000 to her income of £50,000, the whole making £180,000. But on this the palaces, the establishment of herself and the princesses were to be kept up. But the Prince Regent had to furnish out of his salary the additional £60,000 for the king.

When the Princess Charlotte, high-spirited, impetuous and emotional, reached seventeen, it was the purpose of those over her to keep her well under restraint. She was much with her grandmother and her aunts, who liked her, but felt the necessity of strict discipline. Her father did not care for her, and was thought to be jealous of her, so this policy of "keeping her down" was acceptable to him as well as to his mother and sisters. It became a sort of bond of union, and grim cabinets or councils were held at Windsor, before which the interesting creature was brought to trial. When her governess, Lady de Clifford, had to resign, she boldly claimed to be free from governesses, and demanded regular ladies.[1] This proposal filled the authorities with anger and horror, and a council was summoned at Windsor, consisting of her father, grandmother and the Lord Chancellor, who all scolded her severely, her father rebuking her angrily, and the Chancellor coarsely telling her that if she were his own daughter he would lock her up. She bore all this very calmly, until she was alone with one of her aunts, when

[1] She declared that "she would not have an Angel from Heaven for a lady, unless she had the choosing."

she burst out crying, saying, " What would the king of England say if he could know that his granddaughter had been compared to the granddaughter of a collier ? "   The king was now at Buckingham House, whose fine gardens were then quite overlooked by the houses of Grosvenor Place, the occupants of which could see him as he took his walk.[1]   This walking exercise was prescribed by the physicians, but there was a difficulty in finding suitable persons to accompany him.   The queen and her family were afraid of being with him, as they knew not when some sudden paroxysm might seize on him.

When the allied sovereigns were being fêted in London, the position of the luckless Princess of Wales became a matter of serious embarrassment, not only to herself and her husband, but to the imperial and royal guests.   The queen, who was about to hold drawing-rooms and to give other entertainments, had no technical excuse for refusing to receive her daughter-in-law ; on the other hand, this recognition would not be tolerated by her son. This placed her in a situation of almost painful difficulty. The prince, however, settled the question in a very rough-and-ready fashion, as the public speedily learned from a correspondence between the two royal ladies, and which good care was taken to make public.

This announcement from the Lord Chamberlain's

[1] This inconvenience might have been obviated, for at one time all the outlying property came into the market, and could have been secured for the small sum of about £20,000.   The king, however, was disinclined to the purchase.   The gardens have long since been shrouded by a screen of high banks and thick foliage.

office, relative to the drawing-rooms to be held by her Majesty, was issued on May 20th, 1814 :—

" Notice is hereby given, that her Majesty will hold a drawing-room at the queen's palace, on Thursday, the 2nd of June, at two o'clock ; and another on Thursday, the 16th of June, at the same hour. The doors will be opened for the reception of the company at one o'clock."

FROM THE QUEEN TO THE PRINCESS OF WALES.

" Windsor Castle, May 23rd, 1814.

" The queen considers it to be her duty to lose no time in acquainting the Princess of Wales, that she has received a communication from her son the Prince Regent, in which he states that her Majesty's intention of holding two drawing-rooms in the ensuing month, having been notified to the public, he must declare that he considers that his own presence at her court cannot be dispensed with ; and that he desires it may be distinctly understood, for reasons of which he alone can be the judge, to be his fixed and unalterable determination not to meet the Princess of Wales upon any occasion, either in public or private.

" The queen is thus placed under the painful necessity of intimating to the Princess of Wales the impossibility of her Majesty's receiving her Royal Highness at her drawing-rooms.

" CHARLOTTE, R."

The queen received this reply :—

" MADAM,—I have received the letter which your

Majesty has done me the honour to address to me,
prohibiting my appearance at the public drawing-rooms
which will be held by your Majesty in the ensuing
month, with great surprise and regret.

"I will not presume to discuss with your Majesty,
topics which must be as painful to your Majesty as to
myself.

"Your Majesty is well acquainted with the affectionate
regard with which the king was so kind as to honour
me, up to the period of his Majesty's indisposition, which
no one of his Majesty's subjects has so much cause to
lament as myself: and that his Majesty was graciously
pleased to bestow upon me the most unequivocal and
gratifying proof of his attachment and approbation, by
his public reception of me at his court, at a season of
severe and unmerited affliction, when his protection was
most necessary to me. There I have since uninter-
ruptedly paid my respects to your Majesty. I am now
without appeal or protector. But I cannot so far forget
my duty to the king and to myself, as to surrender my
right to appear at any public drawing-room to be held
by your Majesty.

"That I may not, however, add to the difficulty and
uneasiness of your Majesty's situation, I yield in the
present instance to the will of his Royal Highness the
Prince Regent, announced to me by your Majesty, and
shall not present myself at the drawing-rooms of the next
month.

"It would be presumptuous in me to attempt to

R

inquire of your Majesty the reasons of his Royal Highness the Prince Regent for this harsh proceeding, of which his Royal Highness can alone be the judge. I am unconscious of offence ; and in that reflection, I must endeavour to find consolation for all the mortifications I experience ; even for this, the last, the most unexpected, and the most severe ; the prohibition given to me alone, to appear before your Majesty, to offer my congratulations upon the happy termination of those calamities with which Europe has been so long afflicted, in the presence of the illustrious personages who will, in all probability, be assembled at your Majesty's court, with whom I am so closely connected by birth and marriage.

" I beseech your Majesty to do me an act of justice, to which, in the present circumstances, your Majesty is the only person competent, by acquainting those illustrious strangers with the motives of personal consideration towards your Majesty, which alone induce me to abstain from the exercise of my right to appear before your Majesty : and that I do now, as I have done at all times, defy the malice of my enemies to fix upon me the shadow of any one imputation which could render me unworthy of their society or regard.

" Your Majesty will, I am sure, not be displeased that I should relieve myself from a suspicion of disrespect towards your Majesty, by making public the cause of my absence from court at a time when the duties of my

station would otherwise peculiarly demand my attendance.

" I have the honour to be,

" Your Majesty's most obedient

Daughter-in-law and servant,

" CAROLINE, P.

" Connaught House, May 24th, 1814."

THE QUEEN TO THE PRINCESS OF WALES.

"Windsor Castle, May 25th, 1814.

" The queen has received this afternoon the Princess
of Wales's letter of yesterday, in reply to the communication which she was desired by the Prince Regent to
make to her ; and she is sensible of the disposition
expressed by her Royal Highness not to discuss with
her topics which must be painful to both.

" The queen considers it incumbent upon her to send
a copy of the Princess of Wales's letter to the Prince
Regent ; and her Majesty could have felt no hesitation
in communicating to the illustrious strangers who may
possibly be present at her court, the circumstances
which will prevent the Princess of Wales from appearing
there, if her Royal Highness had not rendered a compli-
ance with her wish to this effect unnecessary, by intimating her intention of making public the cause of her
absence.

" CHARLOTTE, R."

THE PRINCESS OF WALES TO THE QUEEN.

" The Princess of Wales has the honour to acknowledge

the receipt of a note from the queen, dated yesterday ; and begs permission to return her best thanks to her Majesty, for her gracious condescension, in the willingness expressed by her Majesty, to have communicated to the illustrious strangers, who will in all probability be present at her Majesty's court, the reasons which have induced her Royal Highness not to be present.

"Such communication, as it appears to her Royal Highness, cannot be the less necessary on account of any publicity which it may be in the power of her Royal Highness to give to her motives ; and the Princess of Wales therefore entreats the active good offices of her Majesty, upon an occasion wherein the Princess of Wales feels it so essential to her that she should not be misunderstood.

"CAROLINE, P.

"Connaught House, May 26th, 1814."

FROM THE QUEEN TO THE PRINCESS OF WALES.

"Windsor Castle, May 27th, 1814.

"The queen cannot omit to acknowledge the receipt of the Princess of Wales's note, of yesterday, although it does not appear to her Majesty to require any other reply than that conveyed to her Royal Highness's preceding letter.

"CHARLOTTE, R."

Such was this strange correspondence, which must have astonished the public.

CHAPTER XIV.

In this year the queen had a fresh trial in the loss of her brother, the reigning Duke of Mecklenberg-Strelitz, who died from a stroke of apoplexy on November 6th. He had had his share of troubles, his dominions having been overrun and ravaged by the insatiable conqueror. At the peace he had been restored and became Grand Duke. He had succeeded his brother in 1794. He had married two sisters of the house of Darmstadt.

It was in the year 1817 that the first symptoms of a critical malady gave warning to this excellent lady that her troubled course was about to close. The usual visitation of exceptional trials and annoyances had tried her health and spirits severely. The death of her brother and the attack on the Prince of Wales as he was on his way to the House of Lords, had much shaken her. She was about to hold her drawing-room, in April, when, in the night of the 23rd, she was seized with a spasmodic attack of a very serious kind. From this she recovered in a few days, but the physician's bulletin declared that it had been a fever, with pain in the side.

The indefatigable lady, however, set off for Eton to see the *montem*, then went on visits to country seats—and various noblemen. One of the Minor Canons of Windsor, Mr. Roper, died at this time, leaving a family unprovided for, when her Majesty showed the deepest interest in the case, visiting the widow, though weak and ill herself, putting down five hundred pounds as a subscription, and helping to raise two thousand. She promised to provide for the daughters, and get the prince, her son, to do the same for the sons.

Ill as she was, the intrepid queen never relaxed a moment, and continued to take her part in the numerous public duties and ceremonials that called for her presence. She heroically bore the burden of the marriages and drawing-rooms that now succeeded each other. But there was one trial which she scarcely reckoned on. Attending a meeting of the National School Society at the Mansion House on April 29th, she was pursued through the city by the groans and hisses of an infuriated mob, who crowded round her chair. The sick and aged lady was not in the least intimidated, only expressing her indignation, in imperfect English, that after her long service she should have been thus insulted. Nor was this the only occasion on which she was so treated. She had gone to one of the Regent's entertainments, and on leaving was surrounded by the mob and assailed—as she herself complained, " shpit upon "—and was with difficulty rescued by some of the guests.

When in February, 1818, Mr. Rush, the American minister, was presented to the queen, he thus described the scene :—" At five o'clock they conducted me to the audience room, which I entered alone. Immediately before me was the queen. On her right was one of the princesses ; on her left another. All were in full court dresses, and all standing. There was also present a couple of ladies-in-waiting ; the Duke of Montrose and the Lord Chamberlain. All was silence," adds our awe-stricken American. He presented his " letter of credence " —with some complimentary remarks, adding that he had it in charge from the President so to bear himself as to give hope of gaining her Majesty's esteem, which it would be his constant ambition to do. The queen answered that the sentiments he expressed were very obliging, " and then conversed with him for some quarter of an hour, putting questions about the United States." She was then seventy-six, and her birthday was to be kept on the following day. He describes the scene. " As I entered the room," he goes on, " there was a benignity in her manner which in union with her age and rank was both attractive and touching. The tones of her voice had a gentleness, the result, in part, of years ; but full as much of intended suavity to a stranger." He then recalls how his predecessor, Mr. Adams, had when presented to her, made allusion to the qualities in her character, " which I came to learn through a good source was advantageously remarked at the English court." After an allusion to the dissensions that had arisen between the nations, he said that no matter what they were, "the reverence commanded by the queen's private virtues had been subject to no such charges, and had been invariably felt by his government."

In the case of a person enjoying health, and not advanced in life, these would have been sore trials enough ; but for one broken with age, and beginning to suffer from a mortal malady, they were almost overwhelming. The series of shocks and agitations that overwhelmed her during this last year could scarcely have been more oppressive. As we have seen, the death of her brother, in 1816, was the earliest of these shocks, which was followed by the attack in the streets on the regent as he was returning from the House of Lords in January, 1817, and it was shortly after this that the first symptoms of her malady declared themselves. She had, however, rallied, and with her usual fortitude took her share in public entertainments, visiting the Duke of Marlborough at his seat of Whiteknights, in Berkshire.

This was followed by what was a calamity for the whole nation, the death of her granddaughter, the amiable and much-loved Princess Charlotte. Having, as we have seen, barely recovered from some acute attacks, the queen had been ordered by her physicians to visit Bath and drink the waters. Three houses were taken at Sydney Place, close to the pleasant " Parade." She was attended by the faithful Princess Elizabeth ; and the good old city—more charged with memories of this kind than any other in England—put on an air of gaiety and festivity which was quite enlivening. It was said that it never was so gay from the number of visitors. Only a couple of days after her arrival (which was in the first week of November, 1817), while she was receiving addresses, news reached her that the young princess had got safely through her accouchement. At six, when the royal party were seated at dinner, Sir Herbert Taylor, her own faithful secretary, as he had been her husband's, being present, there followed an agitating and trying scene. A letter arrived for him, the contents of which were known or guessed. Sir Herbert was called out, and learned from the messenger the fatal news of the death of the young princess. But how return and break it to the queen, who had noted his departure with surprise, being so contrary to all etiquette? But it fortunately suggested suspicion to her. Sorely embarrassed, the secretary could only send in for Lady Ancaster, the queen's lady-in-waiting, who was seated beside her, who with the same defiance of etiquette rose abruptly and quitted the room. Then it was that the poor queen saw what had happened, and calling out, " I know what is the matter ! " fell back in a sort of fit. She however recovered, and two days later hurried back to London to comfort her son Princess Augusta gives her friend, Lady Harcourt, a very touching picture of the distressing scenes that followed.

Writing on November 13th, 1817, she says : " Now, my dearest Lady Harcourt, I come to Sunday, which was a

most dreadful day. William's (Duke of Clarence) kindness
I never can forget. His feelings were so natural, so
unaffected, and yet so keen ; speaking of what his
brother must suffer : his then trying to talk to the
queen upon various subjects, without fussing or worrying her—really his sweet attentions to her were more
like those of a woman. Well, then, after talking together
till we did not know what we said, for we were all
stunned, at last the poor prince arrived. He was quite
green and yellow. He put us all so much in mind of the
darling, stopping his tears to tell us all—not omitting
to say often and often, how thankful he was that poor
Charlotte had told him repeatedly how perfectly happy
she was."

After some weeks' interval the queen and her family
were able to return to resume the course of waters, and
distract themselves as they could.

But what must have increased the agitations of this
closing period of the queen's life was the sudden and
feverish haste with which quite a number of her children's
marriages were hurried on. In the year before her death
Princess Mary was married to the Duke of Gloucester, and
during the four or five before the event no less than four
of these family marriages took place. The Duke of Cambridge espoused a Princess of Hesse ; Princess Elizabeth,
the Prince of Homburg ; the Duke of Clarence, the
Princess Adelaide of Saxe Meiningen ; and the Duke of
Kent, the Princess Victoria of Leiningen. We may
conceive of the dissensions and debates that these

alliances must have entailed, through which the dying queen bore herself with her old fortitude, and she was present at nearly all. The Dukes of Clarence and Kent were married in July in the old Kew palace, in the queen's drawing-room that looks out on the fair gardens—those rooms which, bare of everything, we can now walk through, and call up these ghostly royalties. At this time it was noted that there were no less than seven royal duchesses at court, and it was pronounced that the best-looking was the Duchess of Kent.

Another harassing business was the inquiry into the behaviour of the Princess of Wales, now coming to a crisis, with "Milan commissions" hunting up evidence abroad, &c.—a dreadful "worry" for all concerned, notably for the poor queen.

The marriage of Princess Elizabeth with the Prince of Homburg was not altogether popular, owing to the rather unattractive figure of the bridegroom. This potentate was a very stout and unwieldy personage. Princess Elizabeth was herself inclined to stoutness. The marriage indeed seemed incomprehensible, and was universally "quizzed and condemned." To the queen herself it was unacceptable; but though she opposed it, she at last gave way, as her daughter had set her mind upon it.

It may be suspected that the poor princess was eager to welcome the one chance of escape from the life of gloom and misery which had been her lot for so many years, even though she must have seen that her mother's death could not be far off.

Mr. Rush, the American minister, was present at Princess Elizabeth's marriage, and in a very sympathetic fashion describes the scene, which was not unpathetic. He seems to have been most attracted by the figure of the queen, so heroically taking her part in it.

He writes on April 8th, 1818 :—"The Princess Elizabeth was married last evening to the Prince of Hesse-Homburg. The regent was not there, being ill. Our invitation was from the queen, given through the Earl of Winchilsea. The ceremony took place in the throne-room. After the bride and bridegroom set off for Windsor the company remained. The evening passed in high ceremony without exceeding social ease. The bearing of the queen deserves special mention. This venerable personage, the head of a large family— her children then clustering about her—the female head of a great empire, in the seventy-sixth year of her age, went the rounds of the company, speaking to all. There was a kindness in her manner from which time had struck away useless forms."

CHAPTER XV.

ALL these ceremonials were serious trials for the aged lady, who, though ill and suffering, would still gallantly rally her strength, to go through her probation. The same spirit animated her through all the stages of her last illness, which was now impending. She wished much to be near the king at Windsor, so that she could go out of life beside her old companion of fifty years and more ; and by way of making the first stage, set off for Kew, where she halted, but which she was destined not to leave. No house is so bound up with her fitful course, or had so many tragic associations. It was the scene of many an exciting episode, and seems to embody her life. It has lately been thrown open to the public, and the visitors to Kew Gardens can roam freely through all its chambers. Externally it looks modern enough.

A date is over the door—1631. The rooms are pleasantly old-fashioned and well designed, with low ceilings, panelled walls, deeply recessed seats in the windows, narrow, short flights of stairs, and well-carved banisters.   There is a general lightsome air, owing to everything being painted in white.   But we can have no idea of the effect without, in imagination, supplying carpets and furniture.

Here are the old cupboards, recesses, &c.; there, on the ground floor, are the king's rooms (every room is duly labelled), the bright breakfast and dining rooms.   Above, on the drawing-room floor, is the queen's room, still decorated with faded "samplers," and some lean and dingy bits of embroidery.[1] On the whole the place seems quite unattractive, and draws but few visitors, and it would be well if a collection were made—gathered from the palaces—of portraits, autographs, furniture, and other objects that had once belonged to the king and his family.   There should be plenty of such things about.

Here are the little dark passages, with cupboards off them—the maids' rooms—which, in the lack of accommodation, were allotted to the maids of honour and other ladies.

And here, no doubt, was the Schwellenberg's room, and the tea-room, where she presided and received the equerries, Colonel " Fairly " and others.   We can see the Prince of Wales, who had taken the command at the time of his father's illness, going round with a piece of chalk and writing the names of the persons on

[1] In this room the aged queen, within a few weeks of her death, sat erect, and witnessed the marriages of her two sons, the Dukes of Kent and Clarence.   Kew Gardens were then the royal gardens, and there was tea after the ceremony in one of the small houses in the grounds.

the doors. And a most curious feeling it is to look out on the gardens, a most pleasing view of which can be had from the windows. It seems like looking forth from some cheerful roomy country house, for it does not deserve the title of palace, and there are many good houses close by just as large.

The most curious feature is the forlorn solitude of the old palace. Though it was a Sunday and the gardens were crowded, no one seemed to care for the place or for its royal ghosts, or to know anything about them ; its doors, thrown wide open, attracted few visitors; a stray commissionaire looked on gloomily.

In July the queen found herself better, as she fancied, and went out for a drive, but was taken ill. The carriage had to be stopped, and the suffering lady was brought back at a slow pace. By the exertions of the doctors she was fitted to go through the last of these rather lugubrious weddings—those of the Dukes of Clarence and Kent.

By August she had improved, and again began to dream of going to Windsor, but a fresh attack came on, which, however, " subsided," we are told, " through the skill and exertions of her Majesty's physicians."

A great comfort was the arrival of letters from her newly-married daughter, the Princess of Hesse-Homburg. During this crisis nothing could exceed the affectionate anxiety of such of her children as were at a distance, who received, through the channel of the faithful Lady Harcourt, constant reports of their mother's state.

One wrote that she had small hopes of seeing her sister, though she was sure "we should be better together when the dreadful event takes place.

"In few countries people meet with such an example as that set before them by the queen and my most amiable, good sisters who have sacrificed every earthly comfort to attend to their aged parents and contribute to make their lives pleasant.

"You are, dear Lady Harcourt, perfectly right in saying that the queen is the great link of the chain ; and I fear, should one drop off, that much misery would come. In all numerous families there are a variety of opinions, which are softened when there is a person at the head of them whom all look up to. Through their influence a sort of friendly unanimity is preserved ; but should they fail, all draw different ways, and outward union is no more thought of.

"The more I reflect on Mary's situation and mine, the more I regret my other sisters not having been equally fortunate ; as I am convinced they would all have been happier had they been properly established; and they are so good and amiable in their different ways, that they would have been a blessing in every family.

"I hope you will forgive the incoherency of this scrawl, but my heart is so full that I can hardly do anything but 'cry or pray. Indeed, I am generally a melancholy being since the death of my husband."

She wrote again to her friend on October 28th : "There was dreadful news from England, and no hopes of my dear mother's ever leaving Kew. Her being there from the beginning vexed me, as I looked on the place as very un-wholesome and damp. Most deeply do I trust will every branch of our family feel your great kindness in staying with the queen at such a time ; your presence is a cordial to them all, and a real source of comfort to poor Augusta, who from her great shyness stands more in need of a real steady friend than the rest of her sisters. The account you are so good as to give me of Mary's character gives me great satisfaction. I always thought her mild, good, and amiable, but was less intimate with her than with my other sisters. I trust that her good heart will lead her to exert her influence with the regent for the advantage of Augusta and Sophia, who, I hope, will determine on having separate establishments, as, though both amiable, their dispositions and tastes are too different for them to be perfectly comfortable if they were to live together."

On November 13th : "The gracious, affectionate mes-sage our dear mother has sent us is calculated to soothe our minds and to make us all doubly feel the very severe loss she will be, not only to her afflicted children, but also to the nation.

" The resignation and courage with which she has bore her being acquainted with her very precarious situation is a great comfort to me, as I was quite wretched at her leaving this world without her mind being prepared for the awful change—not that I am not convinced of the mercy of God to all His creatures, and particularly to a being who has led so exemplary a life as the dear queen ; but still the most innocent soul must be anxious to devote some time to prayer before they expire, and to take leave of their children."

"My dearest Lady Harcourt," wrote the Princess Royal, Queen Dowager of Wurtemburg, on September 17th, "the attachment you have ever, my dear madam, proved to my mother, must endear you to all her children ; and it is a great comfort to me to think you are with her." She was also glad to learn " that the regent is so very dutiful to the queen and kind to my sisters. . . . I regret much the queen's not being able to see my brothers, and I think it a dreadful symptom. I join with you, dearest Lady Harcourt, in looking on the day that will deprive us of the best of mothers as a most fatal one for Great Britain. Certainly the queen's example has done inconceivable good, and I am the more convinced of this by seeing daily how much is done by those whose intentions are not bad, but from being quite inconsiderate, and from the desire of enlarging their circle, admit all sorts of people into their society.

" It grieves me to hear that poor, dear Sophia is so seriously ill, and I fear she will not long survive our beloved mother."

The Princesses Mary and Augusta were always with their mother, attending her almost day and night, and Lady Harcourt finished a long course of devotion by her most constant and affectionate attendance. The Prince Regent, too, showed an extraordinary attention, and was constantly hurrying down to Kew. Fever now came on, with sleeplessness and much suffering, and it was clear that the end was approaching. On the day before her death, her trusty secretary, Sir Herbert Taylor, knowing her courageous nature, was emboldened to suggest to her that she should make her will, and though it was of an elaborate kind, with many dispositions requiring much thought and balancing of claims, &c., the queen did not shrink from the strain. As we can see from the paper itself, it is a most exceptional performance for a person then within a few hours of her death. Shortly after she sank into a sort of lethargy, which was not thought a serious symptom, and Sir Henry Halford was about to enter his carriage to go on to Windsor to visit his next patient, the king ; a sudden change, however, was noticed, and he returned to her bedside. It was evident now that the last crisis was at hand, and expresses were sent for the regent, Duke of York, and other members of the family, who arrived at about ten o'clock. They proposed to remain, but finding that the dying lady was not getting worse, they returned to town. Next morning a fresh express summoned the family, who once more hurried to her bedside—the regent arriving about twelve o'clock. They were just in time. As they entered consciousness suddenly returned, and she greeted her son, holding out her hand and smiling upon her children. The next moment—it was about one—she had passed away.[1]

Such was this long and remarkable life, which, as I think, it would be impossible to follow without feeling admiration and respect. When we consider the series of trying situations in which she was so constantly placed, we find but little that can be censured. On the contrary, we find steady principle, an unvarying restraint, good sense and warm affection. Many years after her death an unworthy attack was made upon her memory, embodying all the vulgar topics of abuse—German narrow-mindedness, stinginess, hatred, &c. This *may* have been the work of Brougham, but it drew forth an admirable defence from her secretary, Sir Herbert Taylor—an excellent analysis of character, and bearing conviction with it.

---

[1] Mr. Croker gives this account of the queen's last moments, in a letter to Mr. Peel : " The queen died about five minutes to one. The prince, the Duke of York, the Duchess of Gloucester, and Princess Sophia were in the room ; she had been breathing hard and loud for half an hour as she sat in her chair ; suddenly she stopped and, drawing a long sigh, expired. Her hand fell over the arm of her chair, and her head and body fell towards that side on which she had not been able to lean during her illness. The prince was extremely affected, and they were obliged to give him some cordials to prevent his fainting." Croker probably had this account from the Duke of York. It is remarkable that she and two of her sons should have died in their chairs. The remains lay in state on December 1st, at Kew Palace. On the following day the funeral took place at about seven o'clock in the evening—a picturesque spectacle, carried out by torchlight. The procession set out from Frogmore to St. George's, Windsor, where the body of the venerated, much-tried lady, at last found rest in the royal vault.

"Queen Charlotte," he says,[1] "was a woman of excellent sense, and though her qualities were not brilliant, and had not been improved by early education, she had since acquired a general knowledge of most subjects which form the ordinary topics of general conversation. Her intercourse with many persons of information and talents enabled her to take a fair share in general conversation. Nor did she ever commit herself by what she said. She came to England with many German prejudices, which do not seem to have been entirely shaken off. I admit that she was plain in person, and that age, frequent childbirth and infirmities had destroyed the symmetry of a figure which those who had seen her Majesty on her arrival in England described to me in favourable terms. I deny that her manners and disposition rendered her unamiable. On the contrary, those who approached her found her courteous and obliging, and surprise was often expressed that her manners were so good as to cause one to forget that her figure was other than graceful. She was kind and considerate towards her attendants and servants, most of whom had passed many years in her service. She was ever disposed to encourage amusement and cheerful conversation, but, on the other hand, she adhered strictly to etiquette, and she knew how to check the approach to anything like familiarity of manners or too great freedom of conversation. Her court was most respectable. I grant that it was not a gay court, and if blame attached to the queen, it was for not sufficiently

[1] Remarks on an article in the *Edinburgh Review*, 1838.

considering that her daughters had arrived at a time of life when greater indulgence and some relaxation of uniform routine would have been agreeable and reasonable ; but that uniformity of routine had become habitually imperative, a sort of second nature, and allowance must be made for the circumstances in which she was placed by the recurrence of the king's lamentable illness."

CHAPTER XVI.

CHARACTER AND LETTERS.

NOTHING is more remarkable in the course of this royal family than the affectionate union which, from beginning to end, was maintained between the mother and all her daughters. It is really an extraordinary thing, of which there are few instances in private families, that this should have continued for a period of some fifty years. It might, of course, be said that it would have been more prudent if these clever and intelligent young ladies had been established in life with suitable husbands. It was not until late that two of the princesses were thus provided for, one almost on the eve of the queen's death. It would not be fanciful to trace this to an affectionate reluctance in the daughters to quit the side of their mother in the tide of misfortunes and troubles which recurred with such persistence as to leave little opportunity for ever considering such things. To the last they were the same devoted children, and always found, for a span of nearly fifty years, beside her, comforting and supporting her. Not until the regency came were any of them inclined to set up separate establishments.

The queen, as we have seen, must have been a vivacious, animated personage, taking a deep interest in all that was going on. She was keenly alive to the absurdities and humorous incidents of the social life around her. It might be said that she dearly loved a piece of " gossip," and kept herself well acquainted with all the little court stories that were in circulation. What she observed and what she learned she was not slow to communicate to her intimates, with such vivacious comments as occurred to her. These are marked by much shrewdness and sagacity, particularly in her letters to her forty years' confidante, Lady Harcourt. These amount literally to hundreds,[1] and exhibit a gaiety and good humour that is really delightful.

The queen's communications with her friend were of the most intimate and confidential kind. She opened her heart to her, in a pleasant mixture of affectionate outpourings and " gossipy " details. Her sketches of persons and manners are full of vivacity, and show a light touch, with much acute observation.

In November, 1792, the queen was choosing a new lady-in-waiting for her youngest daughters—rather a sort of sub-governess in place of the faithful Lady Charlotte Finch. Nothing gives a better idea of the queen's good sense and capacity in regulating her household than her statement when consulting her friend on the point. " Lady Charlotte Finch," she wrote, " finding herself of late very unwell, and feeling her strength greatly to

---

[1] The Princess Royal's to Lady Harcourt are nearly four hundred.

decrease, has begged leave to be excused giving so close an attendance. . . . You will see my difficulty in finding persons capable of giving that sort of assistance who will be fit to be both companions and advisers to my youngest daughters : as they are to gain not only their friendship and confidence, but that degree of power to persuade them in doing what is right, and not to appear to be a governess —what, in short, they are not to be. I have ever heard the most amiable character of Lady Mary Parker ; she is described to me as cheerful, sensible, ingenious, possessing many resources in herself, used to a retired life, and well-principled. . . . The attendants I require (for there are to be two) is that one of them always to attend of an evening; and when we are not in town, to come to dinner, to stay and dine with them all day, and when poor dear Gooly (Miss Goldsworthy) is indisposed, to be in readiness to come and attend their lessons and to watch that they prepare themselves in the afternoon on what is to be done next day. Never to pass any incivilities or lightness in their behaviour, and to tell me openly and fairly every difficulty they meet with ; and when I am not present to speak to Miss Gooly, who, as sub-governess, is the only person empowered to direct, and who will ever be ready to assist them with her advice whenever necessary. The salary will be the same as that of the elder princesses' ladies. All this I beg my dear Lady Harcourt to think over, and when well digested, to sound the Macclesfield family whether or not they will agree to Lady Mary Parker being one of the ladies about the young

princesses.   I have secured one already, and am sure you
will be pleased with my choice; but I do not name her
until all is settled, in order to prevent disagreeable
applications ; and I think it right to add that the lady who
I am sure to have is married, and that perhaps the unmarried one may at times be called upon to appear when
an increasing (qu. interesting ?) situation of the other
prevents her coming into public.   All this should be said
and well understood in order that no doubts or surprises
may arise hereafter, nor the attendance looked upon as
too much; for I think it much better that both the
pleasant and unpleasant side should be seen at once.   A
fair statement on my side makes me also hope that
nothing will be undertaken on the other side without full
consideration.   And here I leave off, my dear Lady Harcourt, putting it in your hands, and I am certain it
couldn't be in better. . . . One other thing occurs to me
which it would not be improper to insert in your letter
to Lady M. P.—that of health.   Pray say as strongly as
you can how necessary it is not to undertake to be about
court without a good share of that blessing ; and you ought
to know how to state this point, as both of us are acquainted
with the inconveniences of the want of it in others."

The careful way in which this small matter is " thought
out," the judicious forecast of probable difficulties, and
the business-like fashion in which the whole matter is
discussed, shows that the royal lady was a very capable
person, and could adminster her household in a most
satisfactory way.

She wrote in 1784 : " Madam, I am particularly happy
by the king's commands of acquainting you that we
propose storming your castle on Saturday, the 18th,
if perfectly convenient to you and Lord Harcourt,
and though we shall be a large party, pray don't be
alarmed, for we are all *good friends* and *well-wishers* to the
owners of the castle, but none more sincerely so than
my dear Lady Harcourt's very affectionate friend,
Charlotte."

" My dearest Lady Harcourt," she wrote from Weymouth in 1779, " we have lived, if you can call it living, in a
constant round of company and amusements, a situation
in which reflexion shares but little . . . it is pleasing to
think that the Almighty blesses the endeavours of this
Kingdome to establish justice again in Europe—I always
fear Prosperity will make us forget ourselves and give to
our own power what is due to a greater one."

Lady Charlotte Bruce had arrived with the captain,
her husband, and the queen learned that " her conduct
and civility had gained every lady at Portsmouth, and
in particular that she had *left off her manner of showing
partiality to particular people.*" We are thus constantly
struck by the general good sense of her remarks and the
shrewdness of her observation. Madame de Genlis she
thus sketches : " She brought over with her a new
edition of her ' Théâtre d'Education,' with an additional
volume of sacred dramas which are extremely pretty,
strictly adhering to the text of Scripture, with some small
additions here and there, without which no drama can

subsist." She then gives a detailed criticism of the different pieces. " This shows how judiciously she has gone to work. She has a pleasing appearance, neither handsome nor ugly, a pretty figure, her conversation modest, reflections just, but totally void of all *pretensions* whatever, and what the French would call ' *une figure intéressante.*' I saw her for about half an hour, yet not without great fear to appear before so great a critic, being very sensible of my own deficiencies in everything. She has, like everybody else, two characters—I neither do *accuse* nor *excuse* her, but I own myself a great Admirer of her works."

July 19th, 1785.—She had just received the king's orders to acquaint her friends that they were setting out for Nuneham next Monday. " Oh, how happy shall I be to see the possessors of Nuneham again, and therefore, madam, you will not doubt my sincerity when I say the king never could choose anybody who more gladly convey his intentions than your very affectionate friend "—a pleasing and gracious turn. After the visit she wrote : " Were I to say all I think upon the subject, my sincerity might perhaps be suspected, and therefore I will in a few words only tell you *that you did contrive to make us all feel happy*, which is a thing but seldom obtained."

Her method of conferring a favour is as piquant as it is graceful : " The king orders me to say that he hopes you, dear Lady Harcourt, will not quarrel with him for giving you a neighbour at Christ Church by having appointed your brother, Mr. Vernon, a canon of that place."

Of another visit to Nuneham, she writes on August 6th, 1786: "It is his Majesty and me who is to give notice to Lord Harcourt of the arrival of a *bande joyeuse*, and more *joyeuse* than ever after what has happened. God be praised for preserving the life of the best of princes and of men." She then begs very humbly that she may be allow to substitute the Duchess of Ancaster for another lady ; she also begs to know if bringing Miss Planta and the princesses' maidservant " will not be inconvenient : should it be indiscreet, pray, my dear madam, say sincerely yes or no, and you will really oblige." They went on the 12th August and stayed till the 15th.

When the king's attack of blindness was impending, she wrote with much resignation :—

" You are too reasonable but to feel that, under such circumstances, none of us could have enjoyed anything, and though an exemplary fortitude is shown by the dear king, yet there are moments when he feels most deeply ; and the necessity of keeping up before him is such a strain upon both body and mind, that all idea of any amusement, except what is necessary to enliven him, vanishes. Indeed, my beloved friend, for this stroke I was not prepared : it is a severe trial, I will own ; but as the Almighty directs everything for some wise purpose, I do trust that we shall reap joy from this new affliction."

In 1803 she directs Lord Harcourt to dismiss a servant in this pleasant vein :—

" My Lord, I want you to exert your authority in dismissing my footman Oby, as soon as possible, as his unquenchable thirst has now become so overpowering that neither our absence nor presence can subdue it any more." She then describes how some messages of importance were found in the pocket of the man, as he lay dead drunk in the street, by the Duke of Cumberland. " As I write a tippling letter, I think it not amiss to mention that Stephenson had appeared twice a little *Bouzy*, the consequence of which was a fall from his horse. The surgeon declared him to be at least over dry, if not drunk ; a reprimand to him will be necessary, for should it happen again he must go also.

" Lady Sidney as usual came to Windsor, but is always confined when she is wanted—*the finger, the bowels, the head, the stomach*, are warring against one another, and make her as useless as if she was not here."

Here is a very feeling passage written in 1796 when she had been sorely tried and had learned the bitterness of suffering. How genuine, and yet how restrained is the expression !

May, 1796.—" How many unpleasant things have passed since we saw one another. To know them and not to have the power of assisting and soothing the sufferer is real martyrdom. I hear all sides, and know so many things which must not be revealed that I am most truly *wore* down with it ; and my dislike to the world in general gets quite the better of me, for those who do know one, and those who do not, all take *a tort* and *a travers* and say indeed most cutting things. Our ball looked gay, whether it was truly so I do not ask, my feelings were far other ways; but we did go through it tolerably well: the best part of the day was the end of it."

In another view she describes certain ladies who had just returned from Paris : " Some very much improved in looks, and others far otherwise. Mrs. Eden, by wearing an enormous quantity of rouge, looks much more pleasing, and Mrs. Goulborn, by hiding her fine complexion, loses by that ornament ; the latter is quite formidable by three immense feathers, which so directly run into my eyes when she was presented, I was under the necessity of drawing myself back, and I rejoiced a little in Lady Clements' distress, who presented her."

On one occasion she writes that there is no public news, " and as for scandal or town talk, not much of that either. I will, however, mention that the second Miss Scott's intended match with Lord Down is over ; it is said that the settlements demanded were so enormous that the parties could not agree upon it, and other people pretend that there are other reasons more serious even than the settlements.

" The younger Lascelles, *alias* ' Cupid,' is to marry Miss Seabright. The gay Lothario is to wed the sedate and retired wife. How they will suit time will show, for beauty there is none, nor fortune, on the female side. I do not mean that much of either is necessary for real happiness ; but as on the one side there has always been so much pretension to beauty, I wish there was more money on the other."

She can put a scene pleasantly before us with a few

strokes, as when she describes the English being presented to Napoleon.

"When the first *badge* of English went over, the consul was very curious to know who they were, but the number being too great to remember their names, he asked one of his aides-de-camp. The aide-de-camp said, ' Ils sont assurément ce que les Anglais nomment, Tag, Rag, et Bobtail.' This he took for real names and family. The day following Mr. Adair was presented. The consul remembered only the last name, and in speaking to him, called him ' Monsieur Bobtail,' which, of course, offended very much. Mr. Adair is very sore upon the subject " (1802). There is a sly humour in the last touch that is very agreeable.

In March, 1803, we find her writing : " I have neither time nor spirits for writing. We go on *tant bien que mal*, hoping for, if not better times, at least to come back to what we were ; and I acknowledge fairly that I have every day more reason to adore Providence, for keeping us in ignorance of what is to come, as I am perfectly sure that with our best endeavours to prepare for it, we should miss our aim ; for our walk within this twelve-month has been in a maze : but *n'importe*, I will go on, do my duty, and endeavour not to forfeit the good opinion of those I love."

Of Andreossi, Napoleon's envoy, she gives this sketch : " I have seen this ambassador, who displeased me more than anybody I ever saw, for he had break-fasted upon onions, and the smell he brought with him into the room and left behind him will leave an ever-lasting remembrance upon all those who attended me. He looks so dirty that he is quite *dégoûtant* to me " (1802).

In 1813, when the embarrassments from the Princess of Wales were acute, and the queen was in an awkward position between her son and daughter-in-law, she wrote that she would have no more " court days." She supposed she would be vilified. " The world will take it as cowardice."

With a sound judgment and observation she could advise against indiscriminate acquaintances, since she said they all knew that " delicacy of society was never thought of either in town or country. And I am truly sensible of the dear king's great strictness at my arrival in England to prevent my making many acquaintances ; for he always used to say that in this country it was difficult to know how to draw a line, on account of the politics of the country, and that there never could be kept up a society without *party*, which was always dangerous for any woman to take part in. I may be called *humdrum— n'importe*, my conscience is free and I am a piece of antiquity myself."

A visit to Sir Joseph Bankes in 1813 : " I found him in excellent spirits, *looking like ivory*, free from pain, but quite helpless in point of legs. He is rolled about, both within and without doors, and hardly finds time enough for the variety of his pursuits. His present undertaking is, I should think (but I am an ignorant creature), extremely laborious, as it is the etymology of all the old English words, for which he must consult a world of old books and 'dictionaries, and which, with writing down and looking out, gives work enough; but he assures me it is extremely entertaining."

Her piety and resignation to her recurring trials is again and again expressed without affectation or display, and is really edifying.

\In 1809 : " To cheer myself, my dear Lady Harcourt, I take up my pen to return you thanks for your very kind and affectionate letter. I look upon our friends thinking of us when we are under anxiety as one of the greatest comforts. Indeed, my dear madam, we have had an immense share of distress ever since the month of May, about one beloved object or the other ; but some of them are past, and I trust, at least I hope, that I have learnt in that a true submission to the will of Providence. I do not deny it, I have struggled ; but after all, could I have done other than trust Providence, which directs all for the best ? No, certainly, and I do assure you, when I am alone and think it over, I see such singular instances of the hand of Providence in all that has happened, that I must say to myself, Thank God for it."

Here is a notelet she wrote to Lord Harcourt in 1807 : "You talk of loquacity as an evil. I, on the contrary, of *taciturnity* as a drudgery ; for the words of *Yes* and *No* is what I experience daily; and if it goes a little further, I have the history and distresses of the Betties, Harries, &c., of the families. Some people attribute it to shyness, and poor me attributes it to s——ss, and think myself quite a phylosopher to bear it."

In 1804 : " We have led a dissipated, idle life ever since the month of August, and by what you have read in the newspapers, and perhaps learned by report, gay and merry. How it was I cannot tell ; but amidst all this I found the principal person always left out, viz. *Pleasure*, without whose attendance the attempt of enjoyment upon such an occasion is fruitless."

It is remarkable that not merely the king and queen, but their daughters, shared in this affectionate regard and devotion to Lady Harcourt and her husband. Like their royal parents, the young princesses confided everything to these attached friends. The situation seems almost unusual, and unlike the usual relation between a sovereign and courtiers.

Princess Augusta had an unaffected, affectionate nature. The comments of this princess on the various trials with which they were afflicted, her general hopefulness and courage, show what a comfort she must have been to her mother and family. There is a sagacity, too, in her remarks. Her letters are pleasant reading, full of gaiety and lively comment, with plenty of sly underscorings. Mention was made of the delightful expedition to Nuneham, which so enchanted the queen. Of this, the lively princess has given an account so enthusiastic and vivacious, and so pleasing a picture of the junketting, that it seems the best and most satisfactory evidence of the happy relations and unpretending enjoyment of the simplest of pleasures.

In September, 1785, the royal party set out in three coaches from Windsor to pay a morning visit to the Harcourts at Nuneham, close to Oxford. This amiable family were delighted at the excursion. They started betimes, before seven in the morning, arriving about ten, and the young princess thus exuberantly describes what a happy day it turned out :—

"We were met at the house door by Lord and dear Lady Harcourt. We then went to breakfast, and a very good one indeed! And I think I was one of them who relished it the most, though *I had eat a sandwidge before, with the greatest appetite.* Whilst we were waiting for dinner, in the octagon room, Lord Harcourt mentioned to the king that he had a private key of Christ Church Walk, and that he could see Oxford without the least trouble, and that if his Majesty would make Nuneham his home, it would make the owners of it very happy. Papa said, 'Why, Lord Harcourt, it's very tempting.' Mamma, my brother, sister, and myself (not by far the least delighted of the family) kept our wishful eyes upon the king, who fixed his on mamma ; and upon her saying, 'I will do as you please,' he said, 'Well, with all my heart, let us stay.'

"During all this conversation I think our coun-tenances were so *curiously* ridiculous, and I don't doubt that our soliloquys were as much so, that anybody must have laughed if they had looked on us without knowing why we looked 'so strange, so wondrous strange.' For my part I know I could not refrain from saying, ' And O ye ministers of Heaven, protect me ! for I shall be in despair if we do not stay.' However, I was so completely happy when I found we did not go back till the next day, that my spirits rose mountains high in half a second."

"' Thanky, my dear Lady Harcourt ; ' ' God bless you, Lord Harcourt ; ' ' Heaven preserve you ; ' 'You are the very best people in the kingdom, after papa and mamma,'—these were the sayings for the rest of the day. So we went on all day long, and I am sure we shall never hear the last of it; it was the most perfect thing ever known."

Thus this amiable, natural young creature. It will be noted how the family all thoughtfully regarded each other's wishes—the queen the king's, and he hers ; and the delight with which the acceptance was hailed proves how simple and innocent were the tastes of this excellent family.

These joys, however, were alternated with the most gloomy scenes. She was presently to write : "Mamma is wonderfully well, considering all things, and so are *we all;* but though our *situation* is considered *elevated*, yet we feel like human creatures, and suffer and enjoy like human creatures, and sometimes must appear with a gay face when under a very heavy heart, and that is a hard case."

Again, in July, 1804 : " In many things there is great

amendment in the king's state, and in many more not the slightest. There is a vast idea of dress, so very unlike what is natural. I think my father has a *bad* opinion of himself at times—that is to say when he gives himself time to reflect ; at others he is thoughtless and talks of his *youth* and *vigour*, and that he shall no doubt *live* to *ninety years old*. He certainly has a *frightful appetite ;* and that is *not* a good *sign*. The ideas of building continue as extravagant as ever, altering *every house*, unroofing without end to add *stories ;* and the most distressful circumstance is his *fancying* that people have told him things which they never thought of. From all this, my dearest Lady Harcourt, you may suppose that *our life is very anxious ;* but we must submit of it, and the confidence of its being *decreed by a higher Power* enables us to bear *up with it*. My mother is really tolerably well, considering all things, and so are we all."

The underlinings here are oddly and capriciously disposed, and betoken an impulsiveness and excitement that is characteristic. Her account of the Duchess of Brunswick, mother of the unlucky Princess of Wales, is graphic enough, and shows the good sense of which I have spoken.

"I have made acquaintance with my aunt, and nothing can exceed her good humour, unless it be her *imprudence*. She is a very handsome old woman, not a *bit older* than I think any person of seventy might be, but *uncommonly old* if you compare her to my father, and consider that there is but one year between them. She is the image of my uncle who died ten years ago, and so very like that it almost threw my cousin into fits when they first met.

"I have seen my sister-in-law twice with her, and it would be most unjust if I did not tell you that it was impossible for anybody to behave better and more prudently than she did. I really believe her *miseries and frights of last year* have been of service to her. Her attentions to her mother are quite exemplary, but I think they are mutual incumbrances to each other, living in the same house."

When the royal family were staying at Brighthelmstone in 1816, a grotesque scene occurred. The sheriffs of London went down to pay their respects to Princess Charlotte. The regent did not see them, but they were entertained handsomely, and "made drunk" (possibly one of his royal highness's jests), and in that state were presented to the queen, whom they shook heartily by the hand. Then they saw the princess, with whom they were delighted, and on taking leave they assured the queen that they heard in London that the princess was unhealthy and "*very hobbling*," but they thought her quite a divinity, and would say so in the city.

We have seen how interested was the royal family in the "rising hope of the nation"—the little Princess Charlotte—whose situation, owing to the dissensions between her parents, was so painful and embarrassing. The queen was supposed have the old-fashioned strict notions of rearing children—under strict discipline—and

the young creature, full of impulsive ardour, was not likely
to relish her system.   Yet how sagacious and full of true
interest is this letter of the queen's, addressed to the
young princess's " governess " :—

QUEEN CHARLOTTE TO LADY DE CLIFFORD.

" Though I am certain, my dear Lady Clifford, that you
will inform me every day what progress dear little
Charlotte is making in her present disagreeable complaint, I cannot remit writing a few lines to inquire after
her, and to desire you will assure the dear child how
very sincerely we interest ourselves here in her speedy
recovery.   I cannot possibly wish her better than that
she may get on as smoothly as dear Amelia, who got
through the measles without any drawback whatever; and
she would now be out, if the great delicacy of her chest
did not make particular quiet and care necessary.   You,
madam, who have been witness to so many disorders in
children, of course must know that this complaint
requires particular care, and I must name one thing in
general little regarded, and yet of the utmost consequence,
which is that of changing her linen too early, and even
Sir Francis, without my naming it, would not allow it to
be done till near the sixth day.   As you are a great friend
to James Powder, however, I am sure you will not prevent
its being given, as it is of great assistance in forwarding
the distemper ; it did so with dear Amelia, &c.   I trust
you do not suspect me of disturbing either your zeal or
attention upon this occasion—that would be doing you

the greatest injustice ; but my head is so full of fears and dangers of late, that when the heart is full, it will come out with whatever is uppermost. Nor do I mean to question Sir W. F.'s skill. I have now only to add how greatly I wish that you may not suffer yourself from your anxiety, and that your grandchildren may either escape or get well through this complaint. Pray do not offend Sir W. F. with what I have wrote. Excuse the anxiety of a grandmother, and believe me, sincerely your friend.

"August 29th, 1808."

It is rarely that we find a lady of rank and position indulging the costly "hobby" of a private press. The queen, a few years before her death, set up at Frogmore a small workshop, with a printer, Mr. Harding, who prepared her modest productions. These were rather plain, if not rude in workmanship, but her object was by distributing little books simply to do a certain good which she could not otherwise secure. She first contented herself with a few leaflets and cards containing pithy items of information and instruction, simple sheets or "tracts" of a religious or moral character. Such also were "chronological abridgments" of the History of Ancient Rome, France, Germany, and other countries, which were abridged and brought into handy shape for the use of her family and young persons to whom she gave them. There were, however, two works of greater pretensions and interest ; one, a small tome of 111 pages, issued in the year 1812, "Translations from the German in Prose and Verse," and it was inscribed,

"The gift of the queen to her beloved daughters, Charlotte, Augusta Matilda, Augusta Sophia, Elizabeth, Mary, and Sophia," and it was dedicated to the princesses by the translator, Miss Knight—I presume, the well-known Cornelia. Another volume issued in the same year was entitled, " Miscellaneous Poems "—certainly her own work, and containing many of her own pieces. Only thirty copies were taken off—to give away as presents.[1]

Princess Elizabeth had artistic tastes, and there is a large volume illustrated with pictures of her own designing. In one of the palace gardens there is a little temple said to be decorated by her paintings.

Of Lady Harcourt, in 1812, the Princess wrote :—"I look upon her as no *common friend*, but *really a rock*, and

---

[1] There are also two substantial tomes issued under her patronage—and I have no doubt at her charges—which have a particular interest for us. That buoyant and eccentric clergyman, M. Ch. de Guiffardière, ministre de la Chapelle Française du Roi et " Prébendier de Salisbury," is well known to us as Miss Burney's " Mr. Turbulent." For the " antics " described in her amusing chronicle we have little doubt that Fanny herself was responsible, and that with her inordinate passion for flirtation, she led him on by an affected coyness and demureness. He was reader to the queen, teacher to the princesses, and apparently a sober, correct personage when left to himself. He published a French work in two volumes, an elementary course of ancient history, " à l'usage de L.L. A.A. Royales, Mesdames les Princesses d'Angleterre ; " and this was printed at Windsor, by Charles Knight's father. I possess a copy given by her Majesty to Lord Sidney. In his dedication to her Majesty he seems to say that she had a share in it. " Dans le cours d'une instruction de vingt ans, dont sa tendresse maternelle *a bien voulu suivre et seconder le progrès !* " It seems the work of a well-read professor.

privately will confess to you that I know her value to be so great in regard to her affection for my mother, that I firmly believe she has on earth not such another friend. This, however, from motives of prudence, I do not say publicly, not from fear (for I am of too honest a character not to say what I think), but you must be aware that in the *little world* of this house it might occasion jealousy."

Lady Harcourt survived her royal mistress some years. The Princess Royal wrote in this feeling way of her loss : " The friendship I felt for the Dowager Lady Harcourt for near forty years, and which she honoured me by returning, would in some measure have entitled one to express to her nearest and dearest relatives how sincerely I enter into their feelings, and grieve for the loss of a lady I was sincerely attached to." Then, alluding to a memorial left to her : " I certainly required nothing to recall to my mind a friend I esteemed so highly, and whose kindness was engraven on my heart."

THE WILL OF HER MAJESTY.

THIS is the last Will and Testament of me, Charlotte, Queen of the United Kingdoms of Great Britain and Ireland.

I direct all my debts, the probate of my Will, and testamentary legacies and annuities, to be paid out of my personal property, or out of the value arising from the sale of the personals, if there should not at the period of my death be a sufficient sum in my treasury to provide for such legacies and annuities.

My property consists of a real estate in New Windsor, called the Lower Lodge, and of personals of various descriptions, those of chief value being the jewels in the care and custody of (   ), or deposited (   ).

These jewels are classed as follows :—

First.—Those which the King bought for fifty thousand pounds, in the year   , and gave to me.

Secondly.—Those presented to me by the Nabob of Arcot.

Thirdly.—Those purchased by myself at various periods, or being presents made to me on birthdays and other occasions.

In the event of the King, my beloved husband,

surviving me, and if it shall please the Almighty to relieve him from the dreadful malady with which he is at present afflicted, I give and bequeath to him the jewels which His Majesty purchased for the sum of fifty thousand pounds, and gave to me as beforesaid; but if the King should not survive me, or if he should unfortunately not, previously to his death, be restored to a sound state of mind, then, and in that case only, I give and bequeath the said jewels to the House of Hanover, to be settled upon it, and considered as an heirloom, in the direct line of succession of that house, as established by the laws and constitution of the House of Hanover.

My eldest daughter, the Queen-Dowager of Wirtemberg, having been so long established in Germany, and being so amply provided for in all respects, I give and bequeath the jewels received from the Nabob of Arcot to my four remaining daughters, or to the survivors or survivor, in case either or any of them should die before me ; and I direct that these jewels shall be sold, and that the produce, subject to the charge and exceptions provided for in the first item of this my last Will and Testament, shall be divided among them, my said four remaining daughters, or the survivors, share and share alike.

I give and bequeath my remaining jewels to my four younger daughters aforesaid, or in the event of either or any of them dying before me, to the survivors, to be divided in equal shares between them, according to a valuation, to be made under the direction of my executors, to be hereafter named.

The house and garden at Frogmore, and the Shawe estate, having been granted by act of parliament of 1807 to me, my executors, administrators, and assigns, for the term of ninety-nine years, if I and my four daughters residing in England, should so long live, I conceive that these estates being so vested in me, I may dispose of them by will, or by any other deed in writing, and in any manner I may think proper.

I therefore give and bequeath my right and property in the lease and grant of the aforesaid estates of Frogmore and Shawe, with the several buildings thereon, to my eldest unmarried daughter, Augusta-Sophia ; but as the expense of keeping it up may prove too considerable for her means, it is my earnest desire and wish, and my will and pleasure, that the possession of the said house and buildings and estate should in that case revert to the crown ; and that a due and sufficient compensation should be made to my said daughter Augusta-Sophia, for the value of the lease, and of the right and the property arising from the parliamentary grant, and from this my disposal of this property. It is also my earnest desire and hope, that in the valuation of such right and property, due attention may be paid to the improved state of the house and grounds, and of the estates, and to their value as now established. In this expression of my wish and desire, as to the disposal of the house and grounds at Frogmore, and of the Shawe estate, I am anxious that it should be clearly understood, that my object is that my daughter Augusta should receive in money the full value of that property, estimated according to my lease of it, and the parliamentary grant, and with a due consideration to the improvements made, whether it shall please my beloved son, the Prince Regent, to reserve the possession of the said house and grounds, and estate, as an appendage to Windsor Castle, or to authorize any other disposal of them ; and provided also that the arrangement by which the payment of the amount of such valuation is secured to my said daughter Augusta-Sophia, shall preclude any appropriation of the said house, and grounds, and estate, which shall be directed or authorized, towards giving due and sufficient effect to this my last Will, in respect to the same.

I further give and bequeath the fixtures, the articles of common household furniture, and the live and dead stock within the said house at Frogmore, or on the said estate, to my said daughter, Augusta-Sophia.

I give and bequeath my real estate in New Windsor, purchased of the late Duke of St. Albans, as specified in the abstract of deeds annexed to this my last will and testament, now commonly called the Lower Lodge, and its appendages and appurtenances, to my youngest daughter Sophia.

I give and bequeath my books, plate, house-linen, china, pictures, drawings, prints, all articles of ornamental furniture, and all other valuables and personals, to be divided in equal shares, according to a distribution and valuation to be made under the direction of my executors, among my four younger daughters aforesaid, saving and excepting such articles as shall be specified herein after, or in a codicil to this my last Will and Testament, or in a list annexed to it.

Having brought from Mecklenburg various property, as specified in the list No. 1, annexed to this my last Will and Testament, it is my wish and desire, and my last will and pleasure, that such property should revert to the House of Mecklenburgh-Strelitz; and I direct that it shall be sent back to the senior branch of that House.

I give and bequeath, as specified in the list No. 2, annexed to this my last Will and Testament, to be paid out of the value of my personal property, within six months after my death.

I nominate and appoint Charles George Lord Arden and M. Gen. Herbert Taylor, to be trustees for the property herein bequeathed to my daughters, Elizabeth and Mary, which property is hereby left to them independent of any husbands they have, or may have, for their sole benefit and use, and for which their receipts shall be a full discharge to the said trustees.

I nominate and appoint Charles George Lord Arden and M. Gen. Herbert Taylor, to be executors to this my Will; and I do hereby declare this to be my last Will and Testament.

In witness whereof, I, the said Charlotte, Queen of the United Kingdoms of Great Britain and Ireland, have to this, my last Will and Testament, set my Hand and Seal

this sixteenth day of November, in the year of our Lord
one thousand eight hundred and eighteen.

(Signed)

CHARLOTTE R.   (Seal.)

Signed, sealed, published, and declared, by
    the said Charlotte, Queen of the
    United Kingdoms of Great Britain
    and Ireland, as and for her last Will
    and Testament, in the presence of us,
    who, in her presence, and at her desire,
    and in the presence of each other,
    have hereunto subscribed our names
    as witnesses hereof.

(Signed)   H. TAYLOR,
FR. MILMAN,
HENRY HALFORD.

The blanks in the Will were occasioned by the want of
immediate recollection on the part of the testator, as to
the hands or places where the property mentioned was
deposited. Thus also it happens, that no such lists as
those stated by Her Majesty could afterwards be found
after a most diligent search, on which account the
executors found themselves necessitated to make a joint
affidavit to that effect in the Commons, as follows :—

Appeared personally the Right Honorable Charles
George Lord Arden, and Herbert Taylor, of Windsor, in

the county of Berks, Esquire, and being duly sworn to
depose the truth, made oath that they are the executors
named in the last Will and Testament of Her Most
Excellent Majesty Charlotte, Queen of the United
Kingdoms of Great Britain and Ireland, deceased, bearing date the 16th day of November, 1818. And the
appearer Herbert Taylor for himself saith, that immediately after the execution of the said Will by her said
Most Excellent Majesty, it was delivered to him for safe
custody, and he thereupon sealed up the same in the
presence of her said Majesty in an envelope from which
it had been taken, for the purpose of being executed as
aforesaid ; and the said Will remained so sealed up in
his possession until the death of Her said Majesty, which
happened on Tuesday the 17th day of November, 1818.
And both the appearers for themselves say that on the
following day, to wit, the 18th day of the said month of
November, the said Will was opened and read by them.
And they then observed the following clause in the
seventh page of the said Will, viz. " Having brought
from Mecklenburg various property, as specified in the
list No. 1, annexed to this my last Will and Testament,
it is my wish and desire, and my last will and pleasure,
that such property shall revert to the House of Mecklenburg-Strelitz ; and I direct that it shall be sent back
to the senior branch of that House.—I give and
bequeath, as specified in the list No. 2, annexed to this
my last Will and Testament, to be paid out of the value of
my personal property within six months after my death."

And they further made oath, that no list of property as stated to be annexed to the said Will under the mark No. 1, or any list of request also stated to be annexed under the mark No. 2, were found annexed to the said Will, or contained in the envelope in which the said Will was inclosed as aforesaid.

And the appearers further make oath and say, that they have carefully looked over and inspected the papers left by Her said Most Excellent Majesty, and that no such lists as those referred to in the said clauses have been discovered or found by them, or either of them, and they do verily and in their consciences believe that no such lists were ever prepared by Her said Majesty, and that she died without preparing the same, though it is within the knowledge of the appearer Herbert Taylor, that Her said Majesty had signified her intention to prepare the lists as referred to in the said clauses under the marks No. 1 and No. 2, and to have annexed them to the said Will, so as to have formed part thereof.

(Signed)   ARDEN,

H. TAYLOR.

The eighth day of January, 1819, the said
     Right Honourable Charles George
     Lord Arden, and Herbert Taylor, Esq.,
     were duly sworn to the truth of this
     affidavit. Before me,

(Signed)   S. B. BURNABY, Surrogate.

Present—ILTED NICHOLL, Not. Pub.

It should be here observed that the value of the
personal property sworn to in the probate was under one
hundred and forty thousand pounds ; that in consequence
of the verbal expression of the Queen's intentions, a very
fine set of garnets and brilliants has been considered as
a legacy to her eldest daughter, the Queen Dowager of
Wirtemburg, and sent to their sister by the princesses
here ; and that the whole of the wardrobe made and
unmade has been given by their royal highnesses to Her
Majesty's attached and faithful attendant Mrs. Becken-
dorff.

Made in the USA
Las Vegas, NV
24 June 2023

73852816R00184